PETER SHILTON

the magnificent obsession

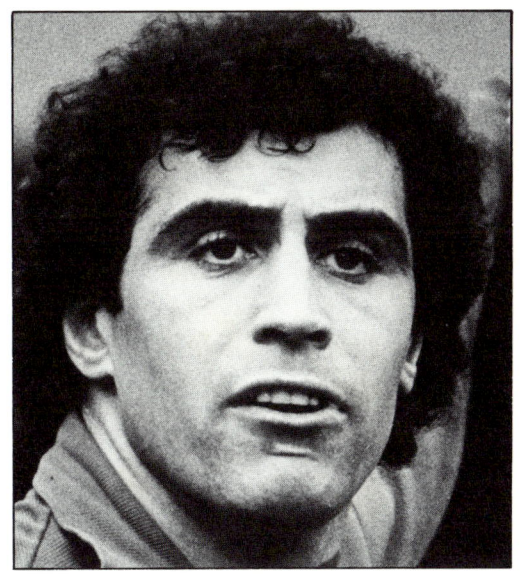

Published by World's Work Ltd
The Windmill Press,
Kingswood, Tadworth, Surrey

Typeset by CCC, printed and bound in Great Britain by William
Clowes (Beccles) Limited, Beccles and London

437 17430 1

PETER SHILTON

the magnificent obsession

JASON TOMAS
with PETER SHILTON

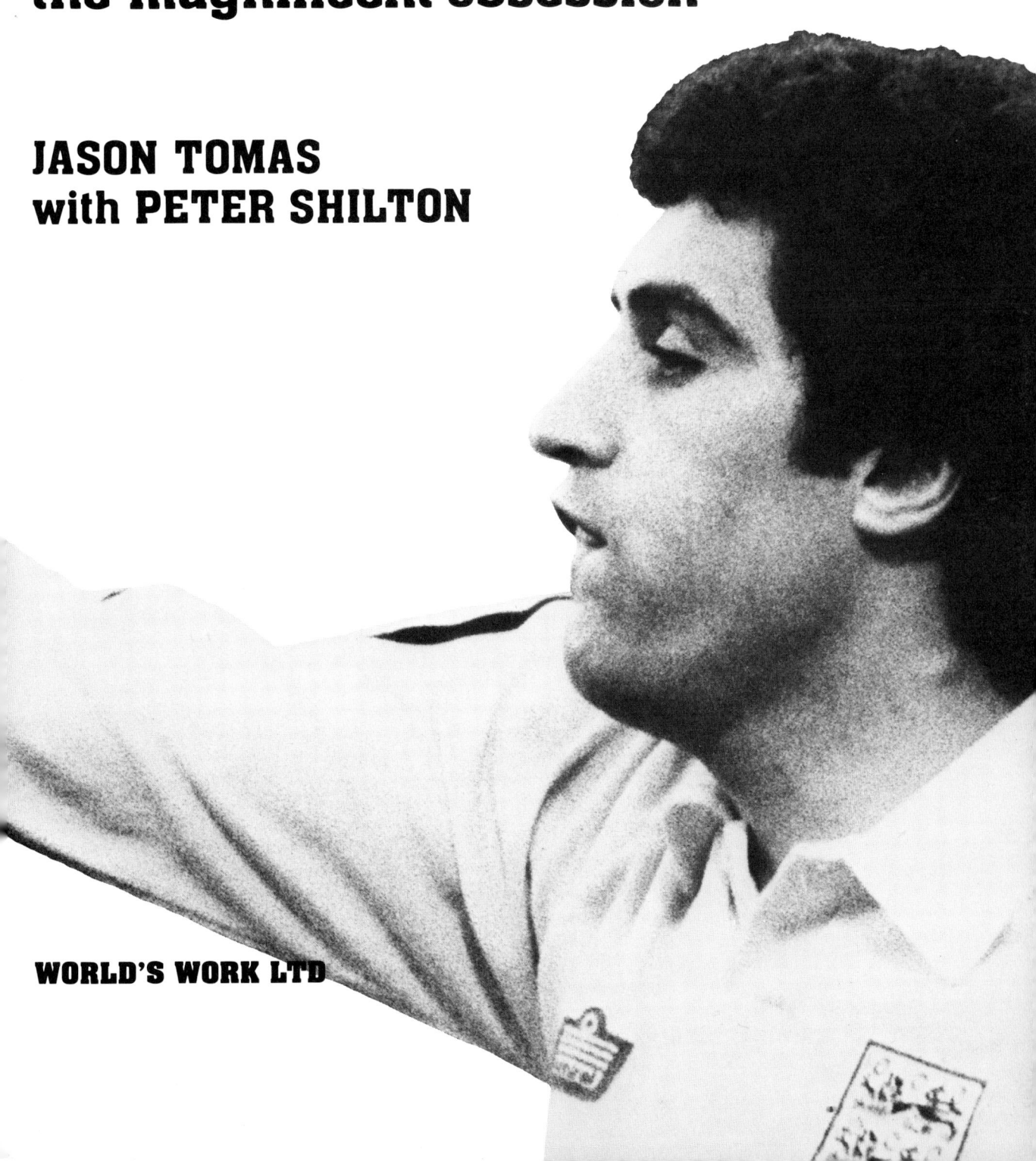

WORLD'S WORK LTD

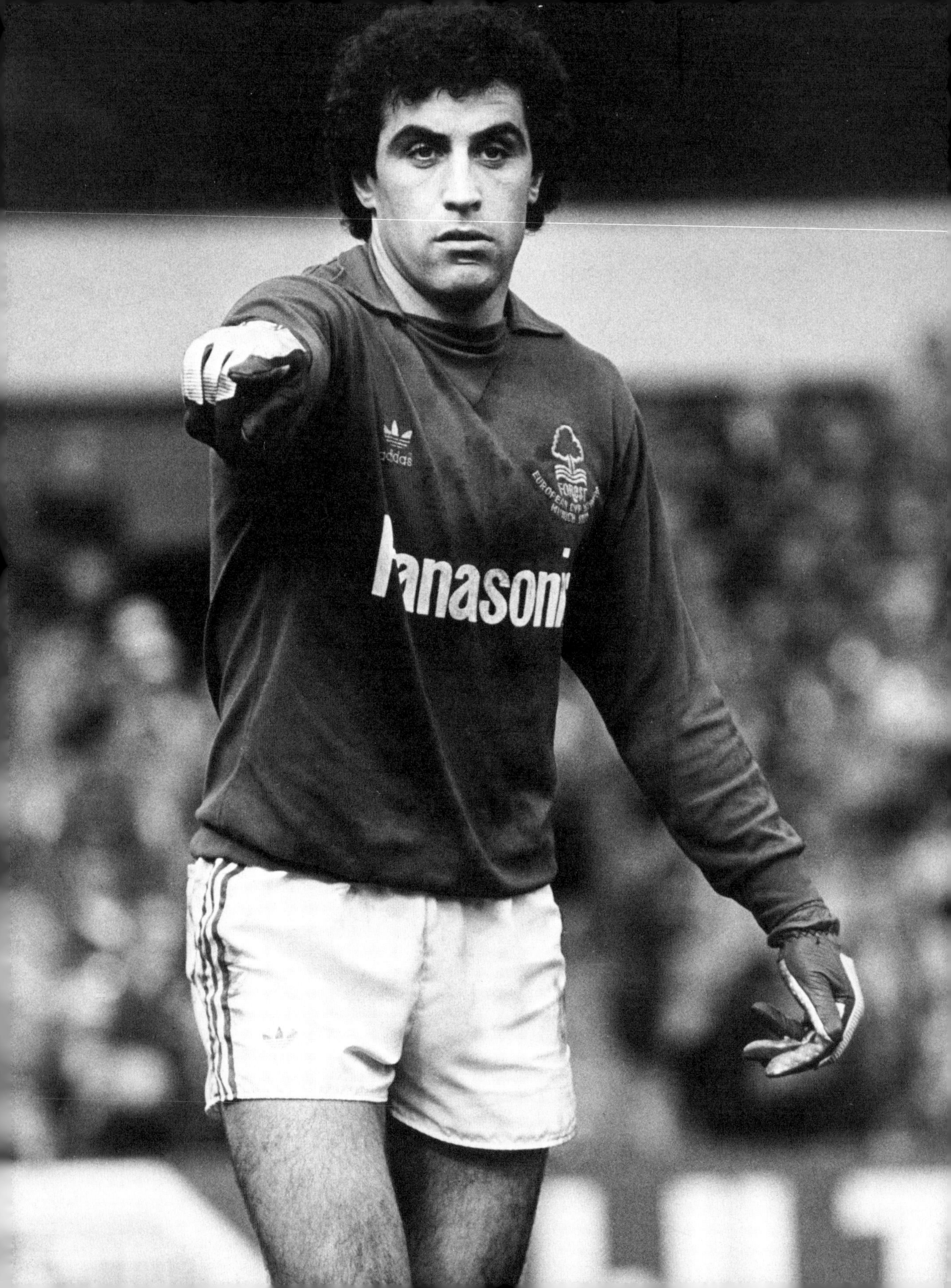
adidas
anasoni

INTRODUCTION

Goalkeeping is a very special footballing art. The goalkeeper is frequently left with little to do but his concentration must never waver. A single quick pass and he can become the focus of the action, the man on whom finally the success or failure of his team depends.

He, alone among his team, uses his hands as well as his feet. He is not only required to be skilful with both but possess the ability of a gymnast, a Spartan resilience when it comes to taking knocks and unlimited courage. Above all, a goalkeeper must have confidence, for without that he is dead. Of all British goalkeepers, I believe Peter Shilton has thought most about the special requirements of his job. As a boy he stretched his body, with his mother hanging on to his legs as he hung from the banister at home. In that single image is epitomised the attention to detail that he has brought to his role ever since.

Thus when I asked him to provide me with his own "rough" explanatory diagrams to demonstrate the tactics and incidents of a goalkeeper's life, page after page of meticulously drawn diagrams arrived with copious notes. Artist Paul Buckle has adapted the cream of these for this book. Wherever one went to talk to people about Peter Shilton, the same impression of intense dedication came through.

I am grateful to all of those who spared time to talk about him and his magnificent obsession, to the photographers who provided pictures, and to Arthur Barker Ltd., and to Eyre and Spottiswoode Ltd. for permission to reprint the extract from "This one's on me" (Jimmy Greaves and Norman Giller) and "World Cup '70" (Arthur Hopcraft and Hugh McIlvanney). Finally, I would like to express my gratitude for the help and advice provided by the book's editor and designer, respectively John Lovesey and Margaret Smith. Writing about Peter Shilton, even with his unstinting aid, has not been an easy task. Just as he searches for the ultimate, perfect save, so he has been anxious to have a perfect book.

Jason Tomas
January 1982

CONTENTS

THE MAKING OF PETER

A great goalkeeper in embryo ... Peter Shilton, at 14, emphasising his star potential for Leicester boys against Chester Le Street in a 1964 English Schools Trophy match.

Peter Shilton was once asked, during an interview for a boys' soccer magazine, what advice he would give to any youngster with aspirations of becoming a professional footballer: "Work hard at the game," Shilton replied, "and set your sights high." It was by no means a profound comment; indeed those words have probably been uttered by hundreds of other leading players. Nevertheless it's one which best sums up the method of Peter Leslie Shilton in becoming, arguably, the No. 1 goalkeeper in the world.

Shilton has taken his own advice to the extreme, to a point where it is almost an obsession and explains why, even now at the age of 32, he is as critical and demanding, both of himself and those around him, as when he first appeared on the First Division scene in 1966.

He says: "There can never be a point when you think you have done everything you've set out to do, because then there's only one way you can go – and that's backwards."

Shilton has won virtually every honour in the game and, in so doing, he has emphasised the often underrated importance of a great goalkeeper to a team. Stoke City acknowledged that when buying Shilton from Leicester City for £325,000 (then a world record transfer fee for a goalkeeper) in November 1974. Nottingham Forest did so when it bought Shilton for £300,000 (then a Forest record fee) in September 1977 and made him the highest-paid footballer in Britain at around £100,000 a year.

Generally, goalscorers are the men who are given star billing but at Forest – and to a lesser extent at Leicester City and Stoke – most of the attention of the fans and the media has been focused on the 6 ft., 13 st.-plus frame of Shilton.

Forest's controversial manager, Brian Clough, and assistant manager, Peter Taylor, are two men who tend to adopt a conservative stance when discussing the merits of their players as individuals. But both have said that Shilton has made a major impact at the club during a remarkable four-year spell in which Nottingham Forest has won the Championship, European Cup (twice) and League Cup (twice). Moreover, Shilton has not only been a regular member of England's squad since he made his international debut in 1970, but in 1978 he gained what a number of players look upon as the supreme personal accolade: he was voted Footballer of the Year in the annual Professional Footballers' Association poll. And hardly a season goes by without his name being included in the PFA's All-Star First Division Team of the Year.

Undoubtedly Shilton has owed much to his natural ability but no footballer can hope to progress as far as he has on talent alone. It's a question of how that talent is applied, and most of the people who have rubbed shoulders with Shilton professionally are agreed that in this particular department he is remarkable by any standards.

Among them are two goalkeepers, David Timson and Mark Wallington, both of whom worked with Shilton during the early part of his career at his home city club of Leicester.

The measure of Timson's talent is the fact that he became the youngest player ever to appear for Leicester City in a senior competitive match; he was called into their first team for a League fixture against Blackpool at the age of 16 years 8 months in April 1964. Shilton later broke that record – he was 16½ years old when he made his League debut against Everton on May 4, 1966 – and while he went from strength to strength at Filbert Street, Timson vanished from the scene. Timson, now 33, had a brief spell with Newport County in the Fourth Division before quitting the game to concentrate on a job in the hosiery industry.

Timson recalls that he lacked Shilton's confidence . . . and single-mindedness. "I don't think there was too much to choose between us on natural technical ability," Timson says, "but there was a big difference in temperament. I mean, I loved playing football, but a lot of the enjoyment went out of it for me when I realised that professional football is a business, not a sport. Peter was really able to dedicate himself to the game, to what he wanted to achieve in it, whereas I couldn't. I had other interests – motor sport, cycling, squash, skiing – and the older I got, the more my views and interests broadened."

Wallington's story is different. He spent two years as Shilton's understudy at Leicester before the latter's transfer to Stoke, and then he too emerged as one of the best 'keepers in the country. Wallington did not come into the English League until he was 19, with Walsall, because he was studying for a PE and history degree. He was recommended to Leicester by Shilton, and he insists that he is every bit as single-minded as "The Master" (Wallington's accolade for Shilton). But, says Wallington, the factor which separates Shilton from himself and most other British 'keepers is an enormous capacity for practical work.

"I think about goalkeeping a hell of a lot," Wallington explains, "but whereas I 'study' in the comfort of my front room, Peter will be out on the pitch with a couple of young lads going through the

BOY GOALKEEPER TO WATCH

LAST season was a poor one as far as Leicester Schools' League football was concerned, for the standard of play never reached a high level and some of the best sides were inconsistent.

The same applied to the county teams which I saw, and we finished up with a very poor County Cup final between Dale and New Parks.

Occasionally Dale, who were always trying to play football, showed some good moves, but New Parks were content to bulldoze their way to a fairly easy victory.

Cup guidance

This was New Parks second consecutive victory, but their display fell a long way short of that which gained them a somewhat lucky victory over a better footballing side from Guthlaxton.

The Caledonian Cup final can usually be relied upon to give us some indication of the type

SCHOOLS' FOOTBALL
by A. C. Robinson

of football we can expect to see the following season, but the meeting between King Richard's and Fosse was very disappointing.

Neither team showed the standard of play seen by such teams as Linwood and Gateway in the past.

Honest endeavour

There was good honest endeavour and little skill, and if these two teams are the best we have in Leicester the standard of play will not reach a very high level this season.

At the end of the campaign,

Soundly coached

Thomas is a fine left full-back, and there are some good half-back and clever ball players among the forwards, for whom some secondary schools are going to be thankful this season.

Last season was one of the worst in post-war football for the Gateway, but there were signs of improvement at the end of the season with some good youngsters in their junior teams.

They should have a better season without quite reaching their former greatness.

It looks as though New Parks will have another fairly good season, and Linwood should easily hold their own in Division 1.

They have several useful players, and can rely on being soundly coached

CLIVE WALKER, former Leicester schoolboy international half-back, now on Leicester City's staff.

however, we did see a really good Leicestershire team completely outplay Derbyshire in the Midland Counties Federation Trophy match at Derby, and they were unlucky not to win.

They played fast, constructive football and were brilliantly marshalled by Walker, the Linwood international, who played seven times for England.

This boy was outstanding with a sound technique in all he attempted. His career will be followed with keen interest by all schoolboy enthusiasts in the city

There was some excellent talent in the Primary Section, and several of the boys will figure prominently in the First Year teams of this season.

I am particularly interested in Shilton, who is, I believe, going to Linwood, and should make the grade as the best goalkeeper Leicester have had since Heathcote, who figured in the English Trophy winning team of 1945-6.

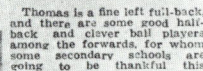

The start of an extraordinary career. It wasn't just as a goalkeeper that Shilton stood out. In the 1960/61 Leicester Primary Schools XI (top picture) Shilton, seated fourth from right, was captain and right-half.

A Leicester Mercury article in the early Sixties on the local schoolboy football scene (left), proclaimed that "Shilton should make the grade as the best goalkeeper Leicester have had since Peter Heathcote." Heathcote played for Leicester when they won the English Schools Trophy in 1946. Shilton was in Leicester's team when they won the Trophy again in 1965, and that year he also gained four caps for England's Under-15 side.

At nine, however, Shilton (above) with his parents Les and May, younger brother Graham and the family's pet terrier "Buster", had all that still before him.

practical side of it. And he'll take it a step or two further: even in training ... if a session has gone badly – say his touch hasn't been there – then he'll remain on the field until he feels he's cracked it.''

It's doubtful, in fact, whether any professional footballer has investigated more thoroughly than Shilton the attributes and qualities required for the goalkeeping role. Such has been his meticulous attention to detail, that one is tempted to suggest that there is absolutely nothing that can happen on a football field which will take him by surprise, nothing which he is not capable of dealing with.

Wallington nods in agreement. ''That's right,'' he says. ''I can remember one afternoon at Leicester, when we spent a couple of hours practising running backwards to get to balls that had been chipped over our heads. It sounds ridiculous doesn't it? I mean, how many times during a season does a 'keeper stand on, say, the penalty spot and get the ball chipped over him from 30 yards? From my experience, it doesn't happen more than a couple of times but Peter wanted to make sure that when and if it did happen he knew what to do.

''It was the same with his punching. I've worked with maybe 20 different goalkeepers in professional football and they'd probably say that there are basically four ways of punching a ball. But Peter has come up with more than 12 methods – a punch to suit virtually every situation in which the ball can't be caught – and spent hours practising every one of them.

''As Peter said, if there's a situation you've thought about that might arise in a match, and prepared yourself for it, you stand more chance of doing the job properly than if you've not given it any thought. For me, that's Peter Shilton in a nutshell really.''

Bert Johnson, the former Leicester assistant manager, puts it this way: ''I don't think the majority of players ever reach their true potential, which is a terrible reflection on the game. You know, when a player establishes himself in the first team, there's a certain amount of satisfaction and sense of achievement; they're earning good money and life's great. There are very few players who want to push themselves beyond that point, as Peter has done.

''What Peter had in mind – from a very early age – was completeness, perfection. He had to look the part, he had to be the part. He was not going to be satisfied with even 99 per cent.''

Johnson elaborates the point by citing the problems outfield players experience when operating in strange positions or roles. Attacking players, he points out, will look comfortable when their team have the ball. When the opposition are in possession and they have to turn their attention to defence Johnson says ''they are inclined to become nondescript and just move around like something the tide brings in and out.'' He suggests that wouldn't be the case with someone who worked on his game as hard and as thoroughly as Shilton.

''We tend to work at the things we like to do,'' says Johnson, ''but are not prepared to work at the chores.''

Shilton is, in fact, a perfectionist in everything he does, whether it's mowing the lawn or choosing a tie for a new shirt and suit. ''It has got to be right,'' is a favourite phrase.

''I've always been the same,'' says Shilton. ''If something doesn't interest me I'm useless but, if it does, then I've got to get really involved in it and everything else goes by the board. I don't like to see things out of place. I'm rather fussy at home. For example, when I come home and the dog's been moulting on the carpet the first thing I'll say is: 'Oh, can't we clear this up,' or something. It's wrong, especially if the missus has had a busy day, but I think that if you are tidy in little things, you'll be tidy in big things.''

While the tidiness trait inevitably makes him difficult to live with and understand at times, Shilton has been fortunate in that those closest to him – his parents, Les and May, and wife Sue – have encouraged it in his approach to football and, indeed, in some ways have been as fanatical in their efforts to help him reach the top as he has been.

Mr. and Mrs. Shilton, a homely, jovial couple in their fifties, both feel that their son's meticulous attention to detail would have stood him in good stead whatever he chose to do for a living. It's difficult to quibble with that view when one delves into his background and sees how this extraordinary character set about preparing himself for a career in professional football as a schoolboy.

Born on September 18, 1949, Shilton is totally different to his two brothers, according to his parents. Tony, 39, is now manager of a petrol station after having spent 15 years in the army; Graham, 25, is a carpenter. Both are married with families but despite living in Leicester and Nottingham respectively, Shilton hardly ever sees them. ''I've never been all that close to my brothers, partly because of the gap in ages, partly because I'm a loner.''

''The difference between our three boys?'' Les Shilton ponders. ''Pete would take his shirt off, fold it and put it away, while the other two . . . well, off it would come, where it dropped it would stop.'' Mrs. Shilton gives a proud smile. ''You could never wander into his bedroom and find anything out of place . . . he's immaculate.''

Shilton grew up in the Leicester suburb of Braunstone, about five miles from the city centre. For some of those formative years, he lived above his parents' grocery shop on a tough council estate. He recalls this as being ''the sort of place where you could put up a fence outside your home one day and have it knocked down by the next.''

The Shiltons were well respected in the neighbourhood due to their business and the fact that, although not wealthy by any means (''Other people in the area thought we were well-off, put it that way,'' says Les), they were well dressed and very well fed. ''They all had big families in Braunstone,'' Shilton's father explains, attempting to make the point about the ''privileges'' his son had without giving the impression of snobbery.

Les Shilton continues: ''Peter was quite a big boy when he was born (9 lb. 4 oz.) and, well, with the sort of food he ate he was like a giant compared to most of the other lads in his school teams. I used to take all of them to matches to save them the bus fare and could get the whole team in my shooting brake.''

May Shilton interjects: ''If he'd have kept on growing at the rate he did, between 9 and 12, he'd have been massive. But he seemed to stop.'' In fact, Shilton started getting bulkier rather than taller and there was a period, after he started training at Leicester City at the age of 11, that people in the club felt he might not grow to sufficient height to become a top-class goalkeeper.

Even at that age, however, he showed an extraordinary capacity to appreciate such problems and channel all his efforts into finding ways round them. Immediately Shilton knew of Leicester's reservations about his height he got some books on stretching exercises. Each day he spent time lying on his father's garage floor and simultaneously straining his arms and legs to touch chalk marks drawn above his hands and below his feet. He even went to the stage of swinging from the banister leading from his parents' grocery shop to the upstairs flat. He had weights on his feet and his father and mother pulled on his legs for good measure. Today, perhaps unsurprisingly, Shilton is two inches longer in the arms than is normal for a man of his build and he has to have most of his shirts and jackets tailor-made.

Les Shilton says with a smile: ''I look at Peter

sometimes and think: 'Oh, he looks like a gorilla – I hope I wasn't the cause of that'!''

Peter Shilton's parents are, in truth, a conservative, hard-working couple, who have built their lives around the maxim that one only gets out of it what one puts in. They are great believers in the old-fashioned virtues of cleanliness, tidiness and moderation in all things. And they are very conscious of ''appearances''.

Their famous son's emergence as a leading schoolboy footballer, his selections for the Leicester and then the England representative teams, meant that apart from being in the spotlight of people in professional football and the media, he was also thrust into a sophisticated world of receptions and banquets. It came as no surprise to Les and May Shilton to see him preparing by studying books on etiquette. ''When he first got into the England Schoolboys side,'' Les recalls, ''I just told him: 'Now don't forget, you watch your manners when you're eating your meal because you're in the public eye.' That's correct isn't it? You can tell some, and it wouldn't make any difference but Peter didn't need to be told. He's like his Mum – she's always been methodical too. Everything she does has got to be so-so.''

The comment prompted May Shilton to recall the day when her son complained – albeit gently – about his bed not having been made. Shilton was a Leicester City apprentice and Les and May, having sold their grocery shop, were running a busy cafe. ''It was 5.30 am until 7.30 pm and looking back you wonder how you managed.'' On one particularly hectic day, when there was a staff shortage, she wasn't able to do all her normal household chores by the time Shilton arrived home from training. ''I was dashing around the kitchen, getting his tea ready, when I heard him call me from the top of the stairs. 'Mum', he said, 'did you know my bed hasn't been made?'''

''Yes, I know, Peter,'' she replied.

''But *why* hasn't it been made?'' Shilton asked!

She chuckles at the memory, just as she and Les laugh when recalling Nottingham Forest's celebration party in a Munich hotel discotheque following Forest's 1–0 win over Malmo in the 1979 European Cup Final. ''All the time, you could see Pete watching us, making sure we were behaving ourselves,'' Les says, self-mockingly.

When listening to Shilton's parents, and the people connected with them during his early football days, it is clear that he owes an inestimable debt to them for having progressed so far in the game. That progress, at professional level, has been due mainly to his own efforts but it is his parents who must take much of the credit for providing the initial boost through the help and encouragement they gave him as a schoolboy. Bert Johnson puts it this way: "The whole family was geared to making Peter great."

Matt Gillies, former Leicester manager, adds: "I wish I could have taken Peter's father and got him to coach the dads of some of the boys I had on the staff at that time on the art of being a professional footballer's father. He struck the perfect balance between taking a deep interest in the boy and not interfering."

"I'm very proud of dad." Shilton says. "He used to follow me everywhere but never got involved like some parents did. Some dads – and mums – would be saying, 'Oh, that's my son,' and be boasting about them, telling stories about all the clubs interested in them. But my parents never did. They never got carried away by it all."

There are many examples of the sacrifices Les and May Shilton were prepared to make to help their son fully exploit his football potential. The most poignant concerns their decision to move out of the flat above their grocery shop and buy a house when Peter was 15. The reason for this was that their shop was next door to a working men's club and Shilton found it difficult to sleep on the eve of a match. "There'd be a cabaret on at the club until twelve," Les recalls, "and then it would be car doors slamming and people shouting to each other. You know the sort of thing. Well, his mum and I weighed up the pros and cons and felt that if he was going to make anything of himself he'd have to have our backing . . . and he'd have to have his sleep."

To some extent, Les's enthusiasm stemmed from the fact that Peter was able to turn the dreams that he himself had harboured as a boy into reality. Les, whose eldest brother Fred was a leading amateur goalkeeper in Leicester and had a spell in City's reserve team in the mid-thirties, also played in goal as a youngster. But he wasn't good enough to command a regular place in his school teams and, on leaving school, he had to content himself with a match once a week for a local butchers' XI. "I was as crazy about the game as Pete is," he says. "But I was never good enough to be anything special."

Shilton's interest in the game really started at the age of nine while he was attending Cort Crescent Primary School. Les recalls, "He came home and he said: 'Dad, I'm playing football tomorrow for the school.' I said: 'What position?' and he said: 'Goalkeeper.' I thought: 'Oh, no!'." Neither he nor

his son can remember why Shilton filled the position although both agree that his build made him an obvious choice at that level. As Shilton says: "I found I could do quite well in the role, and something just clicked." He certainly did. Shilton's physical power and natural ball-playing ability made it not unusual for him to play at centre-forward for a while and then, having scored a goal or two to give his side the lead, go back in goal to ensure that they kept it.

"When he first started playing for the school," May says, "he was such an influence on the team that it was like a force driving them along. It was so obvious that he had that bit extra."

It wasn't just his build that caused Shilton to stand out in those days. It was also his confidence and dominating personality, his willingness to accept responsibility. To outsiders, he sometimes appeared conceited. "One day when playing for my primary school team at right-half," says Shilton, "I got the ball and was dribbling down the pitch with it, shouting while I was running, when the teacher in charge shouted: 'Typical big-headed Shilton.' That really hurt me. All right, I'd got a bit carried away but we weren't a good team and I was just trying to help."

It has been suggested that Shilton set his sights on becoming a top English League goalkeeper from the day he first filled that position in an organised match. But he says: "I didn't have any long-term ambitions at that age. The first thing I wanted to do was get into the school team and then, when that had been achieved, the local area team, then the Leicester Boys' team and so on. "I used to be a bit of an all-round sportsman as a boy, but nothing hit me like football did. Then that was it . . . the whole thing snowballed."

After every match he played as a schoolboy Shilton would spend hours discussing his performance with his father and striving to improve. It was at the age of 9 or 10 that Shilton started trying to master his goalkeeping angles. If he made a mistake during a game it was not unusual for him to go straight to his bedroom at home to draw a diagram of the situation. In this careful way he pinpointed the cause of the error and ways in which it could be avoided next time. It is little wonder that the first two of Shilton's 20 newspaper cuttings scrapbooks are devoted to articles about what he achieved as a schoolboy player, many proclaiming him as a star of the future.

Described in a Leicester Schools Handbook as their "most exceptional (footballing) product of the

SCHOOLS' INTERNATIONAL MATCH

ENGLAND v. IRELAND

Cliftonville Grounds, Belfast, 14th May, 1965

R CLEMENTS LYTTLE STUDIOS   BELFAST

| W. F. Roberts | R. Charlton, O.B.E., J.P. | S. Death | G. Peaper | B. Chambers | P. Shilton | K. Newman | A. Styles | A. Moss | P. Hart | T. W. Saunders | S. E. Tye |
| | | (West Suffolk) | (Oxford) | (Newcastle) | (Leicester) | (Aldershot) | (Liverpool) | (Ilford) | (Rotherham) | | |

| E. T. King | P. Shoemark | A. Evans | P. Went (Captain) | H. S. White (Chairman) | A. Whittle | J. Stenson | I. Watts | H. Clarke (Vice-Chairman) |
| | (Wellingborough) | (Mid-Worcs.) | (East London) | | (Liverpool) | (Blackheath) | S. Northumberland | |

Shilton in the England Schoolboys team against Northern Ireland in Belfast. Others from that team who became successful pros were Archie Styles (back row – fifth from right), Paul Shoemark, Alun Evans, Paul Went and Alan Whittle (front row – left to right).

Sixties,'' Shilton played for the Leicester Boys' representative team at every age-group level, spending two years in their Primary XI (which he captained), and two in the Under-13, Under-14 and Under-15 XIs. He was a member of the Under-15 side which reached the final of the English Schools Trophy in 1965. They were joint winners of the Trophy that year (the only previous occasion they'd won it was in 1947). Shilton's Leicester schoolboy teammates at one time or another included Dave Needham, later the centre-half in front of him in the Nottingham Forest team. Another was Romeo Challenger, whom pop fans will instantly remember as one of the Showaddywaddy group.) Shilton, furthermore, played for England as a schoolboy on four occasions in 1965, against Eire, Scotland

(twice) and Northern Ireland, making him one of the few senior England stars to have gained international caps at schoolboy level.

During this period the Shiltons had a caravan at Skegness – ironically the home town of Shilton's arch-rival Ray Clemence. One highlight of their week-ends there throughout the summer occurred each Sunday morning when Shilton would position himself in a makeshift goal on the beach with many of the adults on the site striving to score against him. Facing shots from full-grown men held no fears for him as he further emphasised when playing for Leicester's Blaby Boys Club in a Sunday League. All Blaby's players were just 16 years old or under, but despite the disadvantage of competing against much older and physically stronger teams they won the League and Cup two seasons in succession.

"We had to take the lads out of that league eventually because someone might have had his leg broken," Les says. "You know what some of these old blokes are like – they don't like being showed up and, as they'd probably had two or three pints beforehand, they didn't take too kindly to our lads going at them for 20 minutes. But it was great experience for Peter. In schoolboy football, he never really had the shots to save. In Sunday football he was making the sort of saves he makes now."

One man who followed Shilton's schoolboy career more closely than most was Jack Curtess, secretary of the Leicester Schools FA for 30 years and now a Leicester City PRO. Curtess, then a school headmaster, accompanied Shilton and his father when Shilton took part in international trial matches. Curtess points out that while Shilton was an obvious candidate for international honours this might not have been achieved had he not had the necessary touch of good luck. Shilton had not been named on the team sheet for a final international trial –England v The Rest – at Maidstone in Kent but was brought into the England side just before the kick-off, when it was discovered that Steve Death, now Reading's 'keeper, had a verruca.

"On that display," Curtess claims, "Peter got his four England caps."

Even then the obsession was entrenched, says Curtess, and by way of illustration he tells of the time Shilton went to an international match in Cardiff as an England reserve. He was accompanied there by the Leicester Boys' team manager and on the return journey the following day they stopped to have a look round Chepstow Castle. There, Shilton asked the manager whether it would still be light when they got back to Leicester. The question was puzzling but it was answered when Shilton, upon arriving at his home, immediately ran upstairs, got changed into his tracksuit and went out for a training run around the park.

Curtess is full of praise for the youthful Shilton. "He never allowed any of the attention he was getting to affect him in any way. So unassuming ... and he's not changed a bit. You know, on the rare occasions I bump into him today, it's a bit embarrassing to still be called Mr. Curtess." He, too, acknowledges the part Les and May Shilton played in their son's success.

When first informed by Curtess that Shilton was in line for an England cap, Les found out who his son's rivals were and Peter and his father set out to study them in action. "We tried to be a move ahead

all the time," Les explains. "I'd say to Pete: 'There's the lad you've got to beat ... You're not good enough yet, but you soon will be."

Shilton was attached to Leicester City on "school-boy forms" at the time he got into the England team in March 1965, against Eire at Northampton. Aware that he couldn't join the club as an apprentice professional until leaving school that summer, however, numerous other clubs were showing an interest in signing him. Among these were Arsenal, who had kept close tabs on Shilton since he was about 12, and Manchester United.

The prospect of Shilton moving to Old Trafford appealed to Les ("What a team they were in those days") but both he and Shilton were conscious of the help and encouragement he had received from Leicester City. Equally important, Les had mixed feelings about the idea of him having to live away from home at such an early age. "No matter how good a landlady is, there's no substitute for home. Away from home a lad can easily go the wrong way. A natter with dad after a match and a little help from mum in the kitchen helps."

Les well remembers his son's second England performance against Scotland at Wembley. "Best day we had. I can remember getting two double whiskies for the wife to stop her legs shaking and I had two myself." Les then travelled to Belfast to watch his son in action against Northern Ireland. He made the trip with a number of the other players' fathers and was somewhat nonplussed to hear one or two of them bragging about under-the-counter payments – illegal under Football League regulations – that clubs gave their sons as inducements to sign for them. "We'd been offered nothing by Leicester you see. 'What's all this about!' I thought ... green as grass I was."

Bert Johnson takes up the story: "Leslie Shilton was wonderful. He'd heard all about top schoolboy players getting back-handers and all the rest of it, but when he confronted us with that, he was almost apologetic. He said he wasn't twisting our arm but that he felt that if there was anything going it was his duty as a father to see Peter got it. We then said something which I think would have been unacceptable to ninety-nine out of one hundred fathers. We pointed out that Leicester didn't do that sort of thing and added: 'Look, we'll have a gentleman's agreement that when Peter is ready to receive money, what he'll have got in his hand illegally he'll get legally.' He had to trust us and not many fathers in his position would have done that."

Shilton's path to Leicester City started at the age

of 11, when he gained two English Schools FA proficiency certificates, one for goalkeeping and the other for outfield skills. In an effort to raise the standard of the game the FA, in 1961, introduced proficiency tests for boys in their final year at primary school. (This has since been superceded by the "Super Skills" scheme sponsored by Coca Cola.) In the case of Leicester youngsters, the tests were organised at the end of each season by the Leicester Schools FA, with independent examiners from Leicester City FC helping out. Shilton underwent his soccer examination under the scrutiny of Bert Johnson and a Leicester trainer-coach called George Dewis. Dewis was to have almost as big an influence on Shilton as his father.

Johnson, with massive understatement, remembers that "We were all very impressed with Peter." Afterwards Les – referring to the fact that Leicester City couldn't sign Shilton on schoolboy forms until he was 13 – remarked that it was a pity clubs couldn't get good players under their wings a year or two earlier "before they got into bad habits." Johnson said that there was nothing in the rules to bar Leicester offering Shilton training facilities and the outcome of the conversation was that for the next two years, Shilton spent two nights a week at Filbert Street, working under the supervision of Dewis.

Officially, Shilton wasn't allowed to be coached by Dewis or any other member of the club's staff but, as Matt Gillies points out, it was difficult to curb Shilton's enthusiasm, or that of Dewis for that matter. Shilton was originally scheduled to train at Leicester for two hours each Tuesday and Thursday night, before the amateurs and semi-professional players arrived after 6.30 pm, but before long he had stretched it to four hours.

"It was unusual to have a boy of that age for training," Bert Johnson says. "Usually you would say: 'Look, son, you're a bit small or young, come back when you're 13 or 14.' We didn't have the space anyway . . . our gym wasn't a gym, just a small area under the stand, nowhere near adequate, but George Dewis used to perform miracles there. He used to have scores of lads there, all kicking balls against a wall, working at little things, and in a sense we couldn't really spare a small patch for a lad of Shilton's age. But he was so good, a place *had* to be found."

"I knew it was quite wrong," says Matt Gillies, one of the game's gentlemen, "but for the life of me I couldn't stop him." After a while Gillies came to terms with his conscience by trying to convince himself that Shilton wasn't there. Gillies would come out of the main entrance to get his car and Shilton would be training on the tarmac outside. Gillies, with a determination mirrored by Shilton's assiduousness, would then look the other way pretending he hadn't seen him.

Today, Dewis, 70, is one of the men in the game for whom Shilton has the most respect and admiration. Though virtually an unknown to the general public, Dewis has commanded respect and admiration from many other football professionals. He started his own career as a goalkeeper, joined Leicester as a centre-forward in 1933 and after retiring from playing in 1950, spent another 20 years or so on their backroom coaching-training staff. He's still there today, looking after the playing kit and doing other odd jobs on a part-time voluntary basis.

Shilton's gratitude to Dewis is evident. He is one of the few people for whom he has displayed any great affection. "I'm a cold person to a certain extent," Shilton says. "I have a lot of feeling, I really have, but I hide it quite a lot. Or rather, I'm not very good at showing it." But when Dewis was singled out for his long and faithful service to Leicester City during last year's annual Managers and Secretaries Association Dinner, Shilton says he was close to tears.

"All the England lads were on my table and when George's award was being announced . . . well I don't know what came over me," says Shilton. "I had to put my head down and cover my eyes. How I held myself back I don't know." Throughout his professional football career, Shilton can recall only one other occasion when he has cried or come close to it. That was on the eve of his wedding when he thanked his parents for all they had done for him.

Dewis, who has always derived enormous satisfaction from working with youngsters, took to Shilton immediately. He gave him as much attention as if he were his own son. "I was bubbling over about him," Dewis says. So much so that Dewis got Shilton to come to the ground half an hour earlier than originally arranged so that he could give Shilton more of his time without other players becoming aware of such preferential treatment.

"He were that outstanding," Dewis says. "A cast-iron certainty to make the professional grade." What particularly impressed him initially was Shilton's agility. "Terrific – he were like a rubber ball. When some 'keepers hit the deck it takes 'em five minutes to get up. But with Peter, he was down and up straight away."

Dewis was worried about Shilton's lack of inches,

along with other members of the Leicester City staff, though he suggests that he might easily have been a successful player in an outfield role. "He could have made a centre-forward possibly better than me." Even so, it was in goal that Shilton really stood out and Dewis, like Shilton's parents, gave him stretching exercises.

He also spent many hours throwing high balls to Shilton, making him catch them at the highest point. Shilton had to strain every muscle for those balls, which were like flighted crosses beyond the far post. He was often getting to them when the ball was almost behind his head. His body arched like a bow and he was off balance. A number of coaches frown upon that and Dewis admits that it frightens him a little when he watches Shilton catch balls in such a way in matches today. "But he *can* take the ball that way."

Recently Shilton was asked to contribute to a series of coaching films on behalf of the Football Association and one of the coaches there, England Youth team manager John Cartwright, told Shilton that he looked as though he was catching the ball too late. "It's not that," Shilton corrected him, "It's just that I am striving to catch it at the highest point and the momentum is taking me back."

Apart from his talent, Shilton also endeared himself to Dewis, for his dedication, enthusiasm and seemingly limitless energy, illustrated in one of Matt Gillies' favourite stories about him. Gillies it appears once took his son, Stewart, to look at the club's training ground on a burning hot summer's day. All the Leicester players and staff were taking their close-season break but they spotted a lone figure training by himself – frenetically twisting and turning, running from one point to another and generally diving around like a playful young dog let off the lead. It was Shilton. "I went over to have a chat with him," recalls Gillies, "and got the feeling after a couple of minutes that he found me a bloody nuisance for interrupting his work."

In some ways Dewis was disturbed by Shilton's willingness to push himself beyond the normal limits of physical endurance for a schoolboy. Dewis feared it might take the edge off him. But the bigger problem for Dewis, a slight, frail-looking figure, must have been finding the strength to keep up with his protégé.

"George would give me shooting practice for half an hour non-stop," Shilton says, "and if the ball went past the goal, then I had to run or jog to get it back. George insisted upon that, partly to gauge how tired I was and partly to give himself a bit of a

George Dewis, the former Leicester City trainer-coach, and one of the men who have had the biggest influence on Shilton's career. Shilton trained at Filbert Street, under Dewis's supervision, for two years from the age of 11. "I was bubbling over about him," Dewis recalls.

rest. It was good for me in the sense that it helped build up my character. I do exactly the same now ... if the ball goes behind the goal in training, someone will say: 'Hold on ... I'll get it for you.' But no, I want to do it myself. I don't know what it is ... when I'm really pushing myself, I don't want to stop. There obviously comes a point when you think, 'Oh, my wind's gone', but it's important to me psychologically to *force* myself to do it. No matter how tired you are, you still have a job to do ..."

One major reason why Shilton rates Dewis so highly is: "He didn't try to put too much into my head. He just concentrated on the basic stuff." But then Shilton probably didn't *need* intensive coaching because he could do that himself. During his early days in soccer Shilton spent six months alone trying to perfect the art of punching a ball. "I would get it right one day, and the next day would flap at the ball. I thought there must be a basic reason why I was not connecting right all the time." It wasn't a question of practise, he found, but of not using the right technique.

Shilton decided that he was too far away from the ball and thus sometimes trying to punch it with an out-stretched arm. "I thought of the way a boxer delivers a punch, the way he moves his body into position and snaps his arm." Shilton immediately added another item to his training equipment – a punch-bag.

The limited training facilities for Leicester City's youngsters in those days meant that Shilton had to use such imagination and initiative continually and it was a challenge which he relished. One of his many self-created training routines, for example, was to get players to shoot at him from poles positioned in various parts of the penalty area, between the six-yard box and the eighteen-yard line. Those poles helped him acquire a perfect appreciation of the positioning and techniques required to stop shots from any distance or angle inside the box.

After a while Shilton had all this soccer data so firmly implanted in his mind that players trying to get the ball past him must have sometimes felt that they were facing a computer.

"When we're talking about the difference between shots from 18 yards and 12 yards, we're talking about maybe a fraction of a second," Shilton says. "And it's this very fine point of goalkeeping that the majority of 'keepers never go into. After the work I did, I felt I was unbeatable ... as confident of stopping shots from, say 10 or 12 yards as from 18 or 20." Shilton was equally painstaking and thorough when working on all the other basic technical aspects of goalkeeping.

"I did a lot of extra training," he says. "The normal thing in the organised training sessions at a club is to go in, catch a few crosses, have a few shots and do a bit of reaction work. By the time you've done these basic things you've taken an hour up and there's no time really to develop your technique, your actual feel for a certain situation. And you know, there are certain goalkeepers who have obviously never tried to improve on various aspects of their game.

"For example, some goalkeepers are said to be suspect when facing low shots close to their legs, which makes me wonder how many of them have set up exercises to try and overcome that. Maybe they're not giving themselves a chance because they aren't crouched enough, or not far enough off their line – all these things are fascinating."

Shilton, during his Nottingham Forest debut, against Aston Villa, demonstrating the advantages of George Dewis's "catch the ball at the highest point" coaching.

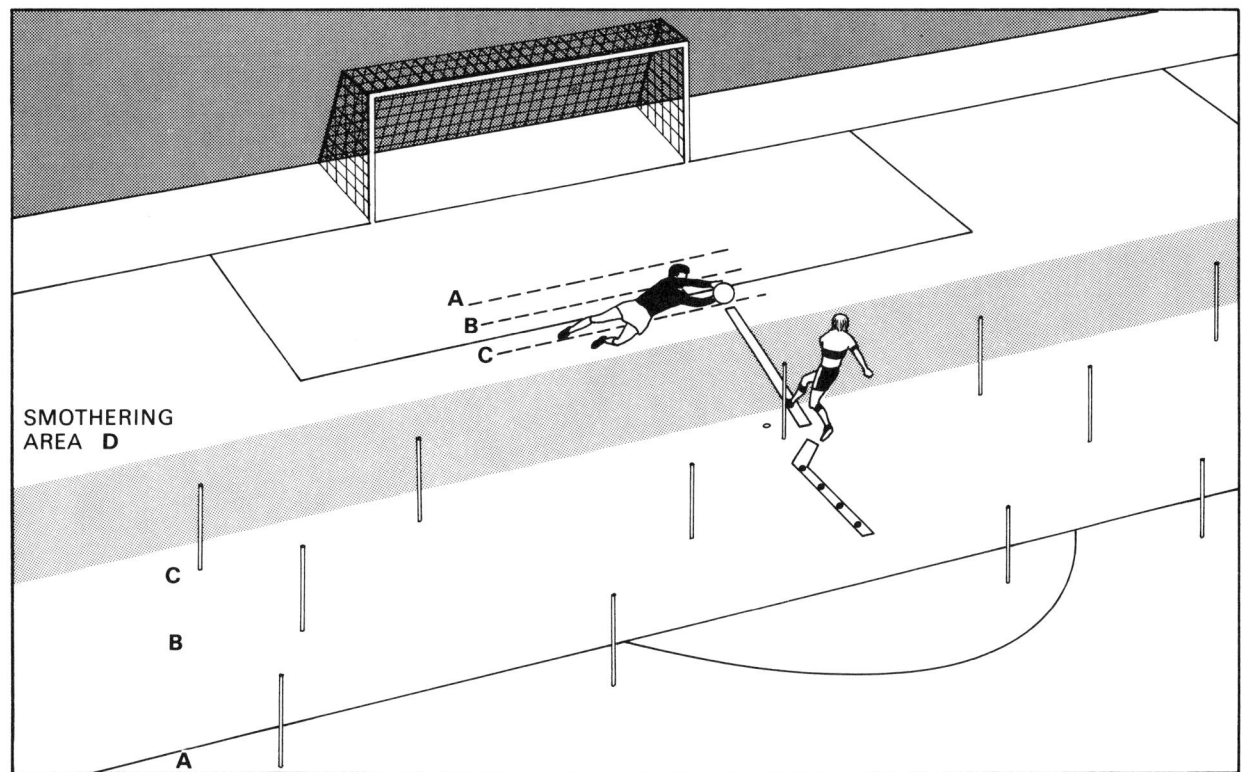

SMOTHERING
AREA **D**

Shilton's meticulous attention to detail in training was epitomised by this practice he created to improve his ability to stop shots from inside the penalty area. He got players to shoot from poles at various distances and angles, and this gave him a perfect appreciation of the positions he needed to be in to have the best chance of keeping the ball out of his net. A different type of save is required for shots from positions A (normal save), B (quick-reaction save), C (blocking save) and D (dive-at-feet-smother save). "It's a fine point of goalkeeping that a lot of 'keepers don't go into."

It wasn't all ball work for Shilton as a youngster either. He'd regularly do strengthening exercises, often with small weights to build up his strength and physical power. He built up his legs and ankles through jumping on and off the small wall surrounding the Leicester City pitch, with a bag of shale strapped to his back, and had similar ways of making himself stronger in the back, stomach, arms and hands.

Needless to say, no-one was in the least surprised when he finally joined Leicester City's ground staff at 15 and became a full-time professional at 17. Not everyone, however, who'd been connected with him was happy about it. He'd been a good student at King Richard III Comprehensive School, where he'd nearly always been in the top academic stream. He was rated a good GCE O level prospect in six subjects, particularly in art, English, maths and geography. But Shilton, who had thought about

becoming a PE teacher, decided against taking exams in favour of going into professional football. It was a move which, according to Les Shilton, greatly disappointed his headmaster. "He was very upset."

Les Shilton refers you to the scrapbooks chronicling his son's years so far in the game. "I'll be quite honest – and I'm sure his mum will say the same – when we put the first cuttings in, we never dreamt it would come to all this, never. That would have been wishful thinking, wouldn't it?"

"It was a little bit frightening at times," May Shilton admits. "He didn't have a social life as such – it was eat, drink and sleep football, and I think I asked him once: "Look, after putting so much into your football, what will you do if you don't make the grade?""

Her son replied: "Well, I've never even thought about it mum. I'm just going to do it ."

2

OPPORTUNITY KNOCKS

Making his mark for Leicester City in the First Division – a teenager with the confidence and authority of a veteran.

When Frank O'Farrell resigned as Leicester City manager, to go to Manchester United in June 1971, he wrote Peter Shilton a letter. The last paragraph read: "If there's a lesson I can pass on to you, it is that opportunities often present themselves without one chasing after them, as has happened in my own case."

To describe Shilton as strong-willed and ambitious is like saying Bo Derek has an attractive figure and that Lady Diana Spencer married into a good family. Shilton has never set any restrictions to his capabilities, the technical side of his game and what he could achieve in professional football. It can be argued that such ambition has proved a weakness in the man as well as a strength because the inevitable conclusion to this remorseless drive for perfection is that Shilton has never felt totally satisfied with life and possibly never will.

The mind reels when one conjectures what Shilton might have gained had he been a professional golfer, lawn tennis player or boxer ... a sportsman in charge of his own destiny. Football, however, is a team game and Shilton has never been able to come to terms with the fact that the extraordinarily high standards he has set himself – in many ways, impossibly high standards – are not always matched by the players around him or the men in charge of them.

The point is readily acknowledged by Matt Gillies and Bert Johnson, Leicester's manager and assistant manager when Shilton started his career there.

Gillies says: "There's a very thin line between big-headedness and ambition, and I think Peter probably upset one or two people."

Johnson says: "If one had 30 players on the staff, it would be great in principle to have them all like Peter Shilton, all burned up about their jobs, fanatical to succeed, because that goes out onto the pitch with them."

Johnson pondered the prospect of a team of 11 Shiltons and then added: "No, it probably wouldn't work ... football's all about balance and mixture and if you had a lot of people like that it would bring you all sorts of problems."

Gillies received a transfer request from Shilton, as did other managers – O'Farrell, Jimmy Bloomfield (Leicester), George Eastham (Stoke) and Brian Clough (Nottingham Forest). Shilton has got on well with all of them but none, with the exception of Clough, provided the platform necessary to completely satisfy his appetite for success.

Talking to such men, the picture that emerges of Shilton is of a man whose ambition has at times

proved self-defeating. Bloomfield, forced to sell Shilton to Stoke, points out that it was during his spell at Stoke that Shilton lost his place in the England team to Ray Clemence. It was a blow which led to Shilton telling the national team manager at that time, Don Revie, that he no longer wished to be considered for further international squads. Shilton looks back on his period at Stoke (1974–77) as "my three lost years."

Bloomfield thinks that an outstanding footballer in a team which isn't among the most successful tends to get more praise and publicity than one in an average or good team. "Shilton didn't need to leave Leicester to become the best goalkeeper in the world," Bloomfield argues. "He didn't do himself a lot of favours. He thought being at Leicester was holding him back, but I don't think he has ever played as he did there. I feel sorry for him that he's not established himself as England's first choice 'keeper because that could have happened so easily if he'd just have let things happen instead of trying to make them happen."

Shilton himself feels that it's a moot point:

"It's true that I was very impatient. There was something tormenting me – I don't know what it was driving me on to certain things. You know, I wanted certain things, it wasn't clicking ... impatient? Well, who knows?"

"I felt I needed a bigger stage. When I first got into the England squad, I envied those players who came from major, successful clubs because they were full of confidence. To them playing for England wasn't any bigger than playing for Manchester United or Arsenal or whoever because *every* game they played was a big game. Leicester didn't get much national media coverage and I wanted to be on the stage of London or Manchester, where if you're playing well every week people know all about it. I thought that would help me a lot.

"It all boils down to trying to fulfil one's ability. I'm a great believer in that. You know, I say to my missus (I put a lot of pressure on her sometimes) that you should never settle for half-way, never settle for second best. *Never.*

"I've seen certain players stay at clubs when they could have moved. They've been happy just playing football and haven't wanted the aggravation and what have you of uprooting themselves. But I think that if you are ambitious, you've got to be a bit selfish. Let's face it, the game is a competitive, cut-throat business and as an employee you're the only one who can look after your own affairs."

Shilton's personality certainly worked well for

him during the early part of his career at Leicester. Gordon Banks, one of the greatest goalkeepers of all time, was Leicester's regular first-team 'keeper when Shilton was signed as an apprentice at 15. When Shilton became a full professional there two years later, in September 1966, Banks, only 28, still seemed set to remain in that position for a number of years. Before the start of that 1966/67 season, Banks had helped England to win the World Cup for the first time. But towards the end of that same season Shilton, already good enough to have made his League debut for Leicester in a 3–0 win over Everton (when Banks was on international duty) and to establish himself in their reserve team at the expense of David Timson, gave Gillies an ultimatum. The Leicester manager was either to give him a regular first team place or sell him to another club.

Gillies advised Shilton: "Give it a little more time to sort itself out," to which Shilton replied: "You can have more time Mr. Gillies, but I'm thinking in terms of days rather than months."

Many managers might have been appalled at the idea of releasing a man like Banks in favour of an inexperienced 17-year-old. Gillies, a thoughtful, quiet-spoken Scot, was nonetheless struck by the fact that Shilton was almost as good as Banks, even at that early stage in his career. Moreover, he was at an age where he could offer Leicester longer service.

How could Gillies break it to Banks, a man who'd been with the club for seven years and was a national hero? "I knew I had to go to the big man and say: 'Look, we can't hold Shilton back any longer, you'll have to go'," Gillies says. "I found this so difficult that I kept putting it off for two or three days." The problem was resolved fortuitously, when Banks, feeling that his game had become "a bit offish" and that he needed a fresh challenge, told Gillies: "If it's all the same to you guv, it might be time for me to have a change."

Thus, in April 1967, Leicester sold Banks to Stoke for the "bargain" fee of just £52,000 and Shilton was launched on a seven-year Leicester career. In that period he helped steer the club to the 1969 FA Cup Final and, after their relegation that season, the Second Division Championship in 1970/71.

Banks, who was voted the outstanding goalkeeper in the 1966 World Cup after conceding only three goals, including a penalty, in his six matches, and who also starred in the 1970 Finals in Mexico, admits that he was a little "taken aback" by Shilton's aggressiveness. When pressed, Banks also concedes that his attitude would have been rather different had he been in Shilton's position. "It depends what you are looking for in life," he says, without a trace of bitterness. "It was said that Peter didn't relax enough, he was too screwed up. I can understand that. But me? I wasn't that ..." Ruthless? "Well yes, if you're comparing the two of us, yes, Peter was more that way inclined than me."

Banks, eventually succeeded by Shilton at Stoke as well as at Leicester (and in the England team too) clearly had an influence on the younger man, although both find it difficult to explain the extent of that influence and precisely how it was applied.

"He'd always be watching you, what you were doing, asking questions and taking everything in," Banks says. "I learned a lot from just watching goalkeepers when I was a lad. You know, when a goalkeeper throws the ball out to the full-back or winger, a lot of people will be following that ball; I'd still be watching the 'keeper, watching what he was going to do while the ball was being played up to the other end. This is how you learn, and I'm sure that's how Peter learned."

Banks is one of three goalkeepers to have made a particularly big impression on Shilton at the start of his career. Former Chelsea and England star Peter Bonetti did so because of his agility and ability to take high crosses anywhere in his 18-yard box. The great Russian 'keeper Lev Yashin because of his charisma. Yashin, whom Shilton once met when Moscow Dynamo visited Leicester for a friendly match, was a towering, commanding figure who played in an all-black strip and portrayed an aura of invincibility, or "presence" as Shilton calls it. "He was like the Lone Ranger," says Shilton.

One of the things Shilton admired about Banks was his positional sense, the way he was able to anticipate situations and thus make difficult saves look easy. Shilton was also impressed by his "relaxed, confident-looking style." But he becomes defensive when you ask him to expand on this. While he respects Banks, as much as any footballer he has worked with, he is irritated that it took him such time to be *widely* accepted as a great 'keeper in his own right.

Banks was thought to have been Shilton's mentor. More often than not Shilton would be described as "The Second Banks". Yet, Shilton says, choosing his words carefully, "I've always wanted Gordon to turn round and say: 'Look, I wasn't Shilton's tutor and haven't had anything to do with his success.'

"Towards the end of my spell at Leicester, I was working with Mark Wallington and when I left for Stoke and Mark took over from me, the first thing I said was that what Mark had done, he'd done on his own. But Gordon never said that about me and deep down I expected him to.

"It's very difficult for me to put my finger on exactly what Gordon did for me," Shilton says. "I mean, I'd love to come out and say: 'Gordon took me aside and said do this or do that', but I can't because he never really coached me in that sense.

"Obviously, I had tremendous respect for him and learned through watching him and the things he said to me, but it was all very general stuff. The thing is, we are totally different people and totally different as footballers. Early in my career, people claimed that I looked like Gordon, which is natural as I did pick up a few mannerisms from Gordon early on. You know, I used to come out and stand like Gordon, a bit casual as if to say: 'Come on and beat me'. But I was only a boy then. After a while I dropped these sort of mannerisms because I realised that my own personality had to come through. I've always been far more intense."

Basically, the way Shilton's personality shines through on the field is that he is more commanding than Banks, and indeed most other goalkeepers. In the past goalkeepers have often been taken for granted, looked on as little more than men to save shots and headers and cut out crosses, but Shilton has done much to help raise their status. Certainly, if there was a Goalkeepers' Lib movement, he would be its chairman. He likes to think that he has added new dimensions to the goalkeeper's role and while this might seem something of an exaggeration, there is a lot of truth in the claim.

"I used to sit down and think that there must be many, many things that I could do as a goalkeeper," Shilton explains, "things that possibly other 'keepers or people in the game had never really thought about before. For example, young 'keepers are told to dominate the six-yard box. I wanted to be *more* commanding and progressive – positive if you like – because that's the way my personality was developing."

Shilton's personality was also reflected in his willingness to shout advice and instructions to players during a match, take on the responsibility of organising his teams defensively. This, he says, is an often overlooked but nevertheless vital part of the game. "There's more to goalkeeping than just keeping goal."

Jimmy Martin, for many years a football writer with the Leicester Mercury, recalls that when Shilton first got into Leicester's team, his newspaper received numerous letters from supporters "about this kid who was ordering defenders around as if he

Leicester City's delight at getting the best schoolboy goalkeeper in Britain was reflected in the expressions on the faces of manager Matt Gillies (right) and secretary Eddie Plumley (left) when Shilton signed for the club as an apprentice professional. Centre is Shilton's proud father, Les.

was the manager". However, as Martin points out, they gradually began to appreciate that Shilton knew exactly what he was doing and that the players in front of him – even the most experienced – leaned heavily on this aspect of the game.

"There were times when it was felt that Peter took too much on himself," Matt Gillies says, "but defenders like John Sjoberg and Graham Cross – much more experienced than Peter – would be more liable to bless him than curse him because, by getting them onto opponents quickly, he could help them do their jobs."

In a way, it took a lot of courage for Shilton to accept the mammoth challenge of succeeding Banks at Leicester. Apart from being one of the most accomplished players in the game, Banks was also among the most likeable and popular. It would have been a justifiably easy way out for Shilton to have moved to another club, and his insistence on striving to prove himself in Banks's shadow, as it were, says much about the character of the man. It was hardly surprising that the Leicester public were slow to take to this precocious 17-year-old with apparently none of Banks's warmth, humour and outwardly, Banks's warmth, humour and humility.

One aspect of Shilton's game, which his colleagues at Leicester found irritating themselves, was the fury he directed at himself whenever he made a

mistake. The slightest error, one which would have gone unnoticed by everyone watching, would be followed by Shilton beating the ground or displaying other signs of annoyance. "Why advertise it if no-one has spotted it?" assistant manager Bert Johnson asked him one day. "It's a bad habit . . . cut it out."

Shilton, however, still shows that self-demanding side in his game even today. "I did it in a recent England training session," he says. "I started shouting at myself. It's a little bit of showmanship but the main thing is that I *am* mad at myself and want to demonstrate just how much I care."

Johnson was also disturbed that when Shilton did extra training the emphasis tended to be put on all the work that *he* wanted to do while the interests of the players with him were pushed into the background. But, in the last analysis, Johnson and Gillies got on well with Shilton because they shared his views on the importance of goalkeepers.

"When I was in the game," Gillies says, "I couldn't understand why so many managers seemed to think that 'keepers were ten a penny. I always felt that a good 'keeper is twice the value of anyone else, even a goalscorer. All right, a scorer will get you the goals to win a match, but a goalkeeper will provide the foundation by keeping you in the match." And

Shilton has emphasised the point at Leicester, Stoke and Nottingham Forest.

Up to the 1981/82 season, Shilton's goals-against average over more than 550 League matches was just one goal per game, an impressive figure when one takes into account that for much of his career he has not been in outstanding sides. His critics point out that he was a member of two teams relegated to the Second Division (Leicester and Stoke in 1968/69 and 1976/77) but in those two seasons he conceded no more than 68 and 51 goals respectively. Shilton considers that he probably had the best season of his career when Stoke went out of the First Division, as far as his own performances were concerned, a claim partly supported by the fact that Sunderland and Tottenham, relegated with Stoke that year, let in 54 and 72, and that Stoke – one of the most attack-minded teams in the country – had the eighth best defensive record in the First Division.

Statistics, of course, can be used to prove any point and so it's when one looks through newspaper reports of Shilton's matches – and the comments that have followed from teammates and opposition alike – that one really gets the most vivid picture of his considerable contribution. It's difficult to imagine any goalkeeper who has provoked more compli-

Three goalkeepers Shilton studied at the start of his career. Left, Peter Bonetti, the former Chelsea and England star, who was nicknamed "The Cat" for his agility and ability to take high crosses anywhere in his 18-yard box. Centre, the towering Russian Lev Yashin, whose build and all-black strip gave him an aura of invincibility – "He was like the Lone Ranger," Shilton says. Right, Gordon Banks, noted for his positional sense and ability to make difficult saves look easy, here shaking hands with 17-year-old Shilton when leaving Leicester City. Later, Shilton also took over from Banks in the Stoke and England teams.

mentary headlines than Shilton. "Shilton's Super Show"... "Leicester saved by Shilton"... "Stoke owe it all to Shilton"... The superlatives have been seemingly endless.

"I've always had this picture of him as Superman," says Jon Holmes, a 31-year-old Nottingham life assurance and pensions broker, who is a business associate and close friend of Shilton. "He's like a comic strip hero, always rescuing kids from being run over; that sort of thing. He *could* have been Superman couldn't he? If you look at Christopher Reeves in the film, 'Shilts' could have done that."

One is instantly reminded of that comment when looking back over Shilton's numerous outstanding matches. Apart from stopping goals, he's one of the handful of 'keepers to have actually scored one. That happened in a First Division match against Southampton at Leicester in 1967/68 (his first full season as a regular member of their League team) when one of Leicester's goals in a resounding 5–1

win came with a high drop kick from Shilton. The ball bounced over 'keeper Campbell Forsyth in the Southampton penalty area and into Forsyth's net.

In that first full season Leicester also drew 0–0 at Manchester United. It was the first time Shilton had appeared at Old Trafford. Despite being hampered by two ankle injuries – a sprain in his left after 30 minutes and one in his right 10 minutes from the end – he made a number of great saves before being forced to leave the field. He did so to a standing ovation.

But it was only after Shilton joined Nottingham Forest at the start of the 1977/78 season that he began to pick up the club medals which his ability deserved. When Forest signed him, Matt Gillies, who'd once been manager there, was asked by a member of the club's committee (it's the only club in the Football League which is not a limited company) whether its £300,000 outlay would be worthwhile. Forest had gained promotion from the

Second Division the previous season and the committeeman, bearing in mind that Brian Clough's team at that time weren't generally regarded as being as classy as their promotion partners, asked Gillies whether he thought Shilton could help keep them in the First. "Oh yes," Gillies replied, matter-of-factly, "because that man will save you something like 12 points a season."

That season, of course, Forest won the Championship for the first time in its history and in his 38 League matches Shilton conceded no more than 18 goals, the best record of his career.

The part he played in Forest's European Cup triumphs in 1979 and 1980 is burned in the mind of any self-respecting Forest fan. In 1978/79 Shilton's European Cup goals-against record was seven goals in nine matches and in 1979/80 five goals in nine matches. It was a run of performances which culminated in an incredible Shilton display for Forest against the more technically gifted Hamburg in the 1980 Final in Madrid, which Forest duly won.

Off the field also Shilton has created a Superman image. He and Jon Holmes have worked hard and with an impressive astuteness to cultivate it, to ensure that Shilton is looked upon as the Number One, not only among his fellow professionals in the English League, but by the general public.

Holmes is a lively, personable young man, who acts as an agent for professional footballers and clubs. He helps set up transfer deals involving players in various countries and exhibition matches. Holmes first met Shilton during the early days at Leicester. A Leicester City season ticket-holder, he was immediately impressed by Shilton's drive, and during meetings at Filbert Street with Leicester City players, it became apparent to Holmes that there were two "leaders".

One was Keith Weller, the captain, and the other Shilton. "He was the leader in terms of talking and thinking," Holmes says. "So powerful . . . everyone shut up when he spoke."

After a while, Shilton and Holmes started working together on ideas to exploit such a quality through endorsements and advertising contracts. Their basic aim, though, was not to make a lot of money. "We always talk in terms of image," Holmes says, "what's 'right' and what's 'wrong'."

For example, Holmes recalls their first serious conversation about the way in which Shilton should project himself. "We were discussing what car he should have," Holmes says. "He'd got a Cortina and that wasn't the right sort of car for a superstar to be driving." They then decided upon a Peugeot 504 coupe. "It was good," Holmes says, "it was different and it was the car a Number One would have."

Shilton later bought a Fiat 132 but he eventually decided he didn't like it because "it wasn't right".

"Get a Mercedes," Holmes advised.

"No, 'Cloughie' (Forest's manager Brian Clough) has got one of those," Shilton replied.

"Well get a Jag XJ6."

"No, that's what Trevor Francis has."

"Well," Holmes said in desperation, "what about a Daimler V12?"

"That's it!" Shilton exclaimed. "Different class."

The same thinking lay behind Shilton's decision to have a run of matches wearing a white goalkeeper's jersey. He was the only 'keeper in the country in those colours – nearly all of them wear green for English League and Cup matches – and as Holmes points out, it attracted a lot of publicity and made people talk about Shilton even more than they did when discussing his performances.

Holmes describes Shilton as the "most professional" person he has ever come across, and indeed this is evident in everything that he does. Take his involvement with the media, which the pair soon realised can play a big part in "making" a player. One of the first things they did was to improve Shilton's ability to "come over well" during post-match TV interviews. Apart from his voice – "That Leicester accent is terrible, isn't it?" says Holmes – Shilton once looked nowhere as polished and confident in front of the TV cameras as he does today. He got over the problem by enlisting the help of a man well versed in public speaking and Shilton put the advice into practice with speeches at various dinners and functions for businessmen. "It was a question of getting him into the habit of thinking on his feet," Holmes says, "knowing exactly what he was going to say and how to say it."

Like public relations men trying to get publicity for products and companies they represent, Holmes and Shilton also made a point of occasionally inviting influential members of the media for an informal chat over lunch or dinner.

To some extent, Shilton has been marketed like a new washing powder or bar of soap, and to Holmes the benefits of this were underlined one day recently, when he was having lunch in a top London hotel. He overheard two people on the next table discussing a brilliant save in a match that week, by Arsenal's Northern Ireland international 'keeper Pat Jennings. "*Even Peter Shilton* would have been proud of a save like that," one of them remarked.

Holmes winces when you suggest that perhaps Shilton has been a victim of the "hard sell", in the sense of becoming too formal, too manufactured. "Look," he argues, "when you're talking about 'hard sell' the inference is that the salesman is a hit-and-run merchant. What we're selling is a damned good product.

"The fact is Peter Shilton is ultra-professional in everything that he does. That's the image and that's what we've tried to bring out. It's what separates him from most other professional footballers.

"He has been a star since he was 15, and has a great conception of what a star should be like. Now, you tell me, have you ever met a really big star who is completely natural? At some point, I suppose that he *has* become a fraction over-manufactured but then I think that's what he's like as a person anyway."

A star needs a stage – and at Leicester and Stoke Shilton didn't think he had one big enough.

Shilton and Leicester manager Frank O'Farrell in a celebratory mood after the 1–0 FA Cup semi-final win over West Bromwich Albion in 1969. The other face in the picture tells a rather different story – it's that of West Bromwich's goalkeeper John Osborne who, in the closing minutes of the match, allowed a speculative Allan Clarke shot to bobble under his body and into the net. "I felt so sorry for John," Shilton recalls. "West Brom had been the better of the two teams on the day and, to be honest, we'd never really looked like scoring. Up to that mistake by John, I was just hoping that we could get a 0–0 draw and start all over again."

His frequently-expressed dissatisfaction at Leicester, stemming from his ambition to get into the England team, began to reach boiling point in 1968/69. That season Leicester, with Frank O'Farrell having replaced Gillies as manager at the halfway stage, got to the FA Cup Final (losing 1–0 at Wembley to Manchester City) but were relegated

to the Second Division. O'Farrell had done a good job and there were high hopes of Leicester regaining their First Division status at their first attempt.

Shilton himself, got an international boost during the 1968/69 close-season, when Gordon Banks had to leave the England squad, to attend his father's funeral, during their tour of South America and Shilton was rushed out as his replacement for the match against Mexico in Guadalajara. At the end of the 1969/70 season, in which Shilton had left no-one in any doubt that he was unhappy in the Second Division, O'Farrell managed to appease him – albeit temporarily – and ease his disappointment at failing to get into the England pool for the World Cup Finals in Mexico, by giving him a new four-year contract worth in total around £25,000, a neat sum in those days.

But 12 months later, when O'Farrell left to become Manchester United's manager his successor Jimmy Bloomfield was faced with the same problem. Bloomfield, too, gave Shilton a new contract, in which the basic terms were the same as the previous one but included a clause guaranteeing Shilton a lump sum if he did not ask the club for a transfer up to its expiry date in June 1974.

Despite repeated rumours to the contrary Shilton did not try, within the period of the contract, to break away. But no-one – least of all Bloomfield – was kidded into believing that when the contract terminated it wouldn't be long before he would again be demanding a move. In fact, according to

Shilton comes to Leicester's rescue in the 1969 FA Cup Final against Manchester City, pouncing on a loose ball to foil Francis Lee (centre) and Neil Young. But it was all to no avail as Young later got the ball past him with the sweetest of shots, to give City a 1–0 win.

Bloomfield, Shilton demanded a transfer on the same day he got paid up. "I gave him his cheque in the afternoon", Bloomfield says, "and within an hour pressmen were contacting me to say that Peter wanted to go."

Shilton says: "I knew that they would never be the best. I didn't think the club ever had a feeling for real success. Maybe I'm being a bit unkind, but in my days there I got the impression that they were quite happy to go just so far."

Shilton does not attempt to hide the fact that his own attitude at times left something to be desired. "Yes, I was brainless, if that's the right word. I let my heart rule my head and needed a lot more guidance than I was getting." He is particularly embarrassed by the memories of his brushes with Frank O'Farrell ("Lovely man, O'Farrell"). "I was diabolical ... you know what I did with Frank O'Farrell? Never forget it. He made some comments about me in the papers and I just went into his office, threw the papers on his desk, and challenged him to explain himself. Don't know how I had the audacity to do that."

On one occasion, Shilton was called before Leicester's chairman, Len Shipman, former president of the Football league, to explain why he wanted to get away. Shipman, Shilton recollects, gave him "a bit of a lecture", stressing the "sacrifice" the club had made for him in selling Banks. That angered Shilton. "Look Mr. Shipman," he retorted, "I think this club owes me as much as I owe them, and besides if you sell me you'll be making a massive profit."

On another occasion, one of the directors at Leicester, who'd previously always supported Shilton, told him: "Even I can't agree with you this time." "Those words", Shilton says, "really stung me."

Bloomfield claims that the fans of Leicester had become tired of Shilton's insinuations that the club wasn't big enough for him and weren't too upset by Leicester's decision to release him. That opinion though, might have its roots in the tension that existed between Bloomfield and Shilton at the time of Shilton's departure.

Shilton informed Bloomfield that he was not prepared to play for Leicester at the start of the 1974/75 season. This was partly because he no longer had a contract with the club, partly because he felt that since he was destined to leave his deputy, Mark Wallington, should be given the opportunity to settle into the team as quickly as possible.

Shilton did make a handful of appearances for Leicester but that was only when Wallington, after appearing in their first eight matches, was ruled out of action through injury.

As Bloomfield says, clubs weren't exactly falling over themselves to buy Shilton, although one of the obvious reasons for that was the size of the fee. The big money in the transfer market is usually spent on men who can make and take scoring chances and Stoke's payment for Shilton – £335,000 – was three times the British record transfer fee for a goalkeeper at that time. The previous highest fee paid for a 'keeper outside Britain, was the £300,000, which Juventus handed out for the famous Italian international Dino Zoff.

When assessing whether to make a bid for Shilton, some clubs were no doubt also put off the idea by the feeling that they might not be able to meet his personal terms. Shilton is never more aggressive than when arguing that goalkeepers are the most important member of a team. This, together with an inborn stubbornness, which can send friends and members of his family reaching frantically for the aspirin bottle, and the self-confidence of knowing he is a master of his job, makes him the toughest of football people to deal with on wage negotiations. As

Jon Holmes points out: "He's always broken barriers in terms of money."

When Shilton left Leicester, his basic salary was £8,500 a year. Stoke agreed to double that to £17,000, but due to a number of complicated clauses, which Shilton drafted in himself in consultation with Holmes, including the guarantee of an extra 10 per cent a year so that his wages kept pace with inflation, it ended up at £22,000.

Little wonder that Nottingham Forest's manager Brian Clough, mindful of Stoke's financial problems at the time they sold him to Forest, opened his own negotiations with the player by telling Holmes: "You've brought one club to financial ruin, young man, you're not going to do it to another." But even Clough was prepared to stretch Forest's resources to buy Shilton for £300,000 . . . and even Clough was eventually forced to pay what Shilton felt he was worth.

Shilton signed three contracts with Forest between 1974 and 1981, the first for a basic sum of £20,000 a year – it was less than what Shilton had been getting at Stoke but he was depressed by his experiences there and desperate for Clough's magic touch. The second, significantly handed to him after the North American League Club, Washington Diplomats, had offered to buy him for £500,000 and pay him £200,000 a year, was for £35,000. The third, signed in 1979, at a time when Clough had decided there was no way he could afford to be without him, was for £75,000 – or rather £90,000 to £100,000 if one includes the many subsidiary and lucrative clauses.

Clough, repeatedly, has been driven to the point of despair negotiating with Shilton and Holmes. During one particularly tense period Holmes recalls Clough's reaction to the clauses that he and Shilton put before him was to tear them up immediately. Holmes is inevitably reticent about providing specific details of Shilton's contract – "It's much too complicated anyway" – but one can hazard a guess that they epitomise the pair's ultra-professionalism.

"I've never seen a contract like the one Peter Shilton and Jon Holmes put before us," recalls former Stoke manager Tony Waddington. "It was a masterpiece . . . the most thorough, watertight contract I've ever seen. I can't describe how complete it was. When you're dealing with clubs and players on transfer deals, the tendency is to keep having to ring up people to tie up all the little loose ends, but not with this one. Everything – to the player's benefit – had been thought of and was there in writing."

Shilton hands Stoke 'unprofessional' rap

By PETER JOHNSON

ENGLAND'S No. 2 goalkeeper Peter Shilton yesterday charged Stoke—the club who paid a record £340,000 for him — with being 'too relaxed and unprofessional.'

The accusation came as manager Tony Waddington tried desperately to repair the morale of a team hit by its second star revolt in a fortnight.

Like £240,000 Alan Hudson, Shilton has become disenchanted with life at Stoke, where quality football has always been put before the ruthless quest for success.

Stoke have won only one major trophy in their history and currently lie seventh from the bottom of Division One.

Unlike Hudson, he is keen to stay there—if the club is prepared to change its Corinthian-style image.

'I am not interested in getting a transfer,' he said. 'I moved to Stoke nearly two years ago because I felt we could work at the game and become one of the best sides in the country.

'But in view of the things happening here I feel that at the moment we are going backwards instead of forward.

'We have the potential to attract big gates if we start playing well. But we'll never do that until we sort these problems out.

'The basic trouble is that things at the club are a bit too easy and relaxed. To be successful we have to be more professional all the way round.'

Refusal

Shilton made his first public complaint after last Saturday's 2—0 defeat at Arsenal. But he claims the decline has been gradual over the last two years.

'Through all that time I've said nothing, just tried to get on with playing,' he said. 'But things have become so bad in recent weeks that I felt something needed to be done.

'There comes a time when it's no longer any good to brush these things under the carpet. We've got to analyse the situation more deeply and do some plain, honest talking.'

Shilton was upset by the decision to make Hudson team captain for Sunday's friendly game in Italy. It was only Hudson's second game since his refusal to play led to the club's first upheaval.

'I believe Alan has the potential to be one of the best players in the world,' said Shilton. 'But I also believe there should have been nine other players in line for the captaincy before him—and I don't include myself in that list.'

Since his initial weekend outburst Shilton has put his complaints to manager Waddington.

'We talked things over generally and I think he understands now how I feel,' he said.

Waddington, who over the years has gained a reputation for his understanding and handling of star players, refused to comment yesterday.

PETER SHILTON . . . 'We have to be more professional'

By the time Shilton arrived, Waddington had built at Stoke one of the most exciting teams in the country and, despite the club's limited financial resources (its average gate was only around 25,000), had spent heavily in doing so. Stoke had already showed signs of becoming a major force in the game by winning the League Cup in 1972 (the first time the club had ever won a Cup competition) and reaching the FA Cup semi-finals in successive seasons.

Waddington looked upon Shilton as the man who would enable the side to realise its full potential, "the last piece in the jigsaw."

By a tragic irony, Stoke's need for a world-class goalkeeper arose from a road accident involving Gordon Banks. One Sunday, in October 1972, Banks elected to drive to a friend's home to watch the TV highlights of Stoke's match the previous afternoon, a game that was not being broadcast in his home TV region. He'd had a foul awarded against him and as it had cost Stoke a goal, he wanted to study the incident. But he never got there. Banks's car was involved in a crash and the glass from a shattered windscreen caused him to be blinded in one eye. He

Shilton's relentless search for perfection, provoked this newspaper outburst when he was at Stoke. "If I see something going wrong at my club and nothing being done to put it right, there's no way I can sit back and accept it."

did make one or two "comeback" appearances but in August 1973 he was forced to retire.

No-one doubted that in Shilton Stoke had found the best possible successor, as had Leicester, but some people in the game had mixed feelings about the transfer fee. Among these, was Bert Williams, the former Wolves and England goalkeeper, who insisted: "One could get a lad off the streets to do the job."

Waddington recalls one Aston Villa–Stoke testimonial match in which, after Shilton had made one or two "non-elegant, fumbling sort of saves" Villa's chairman remarked: "Fancy paying £325,000 for a 'keeper like that." The following season when Stoke were at Villa for a League match Shilton, says Waddington, "seemed to be playing them on his own. I'll never forget that game. They attacked us for virtually the whole of the 90 minutes and Peter was making save after save after save. He dominated the game to the extent that you could see people actually putting more into their shots, trying to bend them, all kinds of things." Stoke eventually won 1–0, through a breakaway goal towards the end.

Being under such intense pressure became a common occurrence for Shilton because Stoke were rather better attacking than defending. In some ways this was good for him because it enabled him to display his extraordinary ability to the full. It was also one of the main factors which helped to turn his spell at Stoke somewhat sour. Shilton feels that goalkeepers need support, like midfield men and strikers, in order to do their jobs properly. At Stoke he didn't get the support he wanted.

"It was very difficult for Peter to appreciate our style," Waddington says. "He felt the game should be played with a bit more discipline but then he talks as a goalkeeper, not as a spectator or a midfield player or a forward. I respected Peter's point of view, but there are 10 other players with a point of view and all these have to be taken into consideration too."

"I think that when you have players with the type of creative skill that some of our lads had," Waddington says, "you had to accept that as their total contribution."

Shilton's reaction is that Stoke needed to score a lot of goals to compensate for their defensive vulnerability. There were too many matches, he says, in which they didn't. "If men are in a team only because of their ability to create goals, and they're not doing that, then they're not doing their jobs," Shilton argues. "That's when goalkeepers are put under pressure and get the blame when their teams aren't getting good results. This sort of thing happens all over the world and it's one of the biggest crimes in football."

It's difficult not to sympathise with Shilton *and* Waddington, for that matter. In Shilton's first two seasons there, 1974/75 and 1975/76, Stoke's potential was clear. They finished fifth and twelfth in the First Division. It was a tremendous achievement.

During this time Stoke lost the services of no less than five players with broken legs, including first team stars Mike Pejic, Jimmy Robertson and John Ritchie. At the end of the 1974/75 season the club announced a record loss of £450,000. The pressure on the directors to reduce the overdraft intensified in January 1976 when Stoke suffered another financial blow; the roof of its wooden Butler Street stand, was brought to the ground by a strong gale. And from that point on Stoke's slide was astonishing.

The sales of key players, Jimmy Greenhoff and

Alan Hudson, in November and December 1976, were followed by that of Mike Pejic in February 1977. Waddington, disillusioned and upset at the pressure that had been put on him by Stoke's directors to break up his team, resigned in March and, with George Eastham in charge of the side, Stoke's disastrous spell was completed by their relegation to the Second Division.

Waddington is adamant about Shilton's transfer request even today. There is no way, he says, that he should have been allowed to leave the club. "A lot of things stated in connection with Stoke's financial problems, due to that Butler Street stand, were just excuses," he insists. "I think the directors lost courage in the sense of not being prepared to keep spending money on better players. If you try and cut your losses in football, you go back."

Waddington says that he always felt Shilton could keep Stoke in the First Division "indefinitely" and that if they had dropped into the Second, his presence would have given them a "99 per cent" chance of getting back. "Selling him was a false economy. It was said that Stoke couldn't afford his wages, but it's a chicken-and-egg problem isn't it?"

Shilton was determined to leave Stoke, however, and not just because, as Jon Holmes puts it: "A Number One can't play in a Number Two team." Shilton did not accept that Stoke's decline could be attributed to just bad luck. The season they were relegated, following a defeat at Arsenal, he caused a stir by commenting in a newspaper that the team wasn't professional enough. He criticised the appointment of Alan Hudson – a brilliant but temperamental and inconsistent player – as captain. He made no apologies for the outburst because, as he says now:

"I get a little upset when I see things that are totally wrong. We lacked a lot of character on the field at times. There was a lack of discipline, with certain players going out onto the pitch and performing for themselves and the crowd and not the team. Things began to go astray off the field too. I, being the record signing, had to try and battle through. It started to affect me because I made two or three silly mistakes, nothing terrible and because of who I was, they were blown up out of all proportion."

Shilton says he thinks the world of Waddington: "A superb manager who'd do anything for you." But adds: "He was too nice a fellow ... not strong enough for what I wanted."

Shilton certainly found such a manager in Brian Clough.

3

LIFE WITH CLOUGH

To get Brian Clough and Peter Shilton around a table to discuss what they have done for each other would be to invite the most heated of verbal battles. They are two men with big egos and, while the chemistry of their innate strong-mindedness has worked exceptionally well during the spell they have been together at Nottingham Forest, it has nevertheless been a potentially explosive mixture.

If you suggest to Clough that Forest might not have achieved as much success but for Shilton's inspired goalkeeping he goes along with it for a while. Then, suddenly, he's provoked into one of his abrasive moods. "Look, young man," says Clough, his finger pointing, "I've rescued Peter Shilton's career. Never mind about what he has done for us, how many matches he has won for us, *I've* saved his career. He has taken his X-amount of pounds a week, with his 10 per cent clauses and all that and I've given him things which he couldn't buy, even if he was a millionaire. I've given him medals to show his children."

Relate that comment to Shilton and he too becomes strangely animated. He has got four of those medals – for helping Forest win the Championship in 1978, the European Cup and League Cup in 1979 and the European Cup in 1980 and as Clough observes, he's so proud of them that "according to his wife, he even watches her when she's looking at them." But while there's a lot of truth in what Clough says about the influence he's had on Shilton, there's also a lot of truth in Shilton's assertion that he's helped Clough become a winner too. "All he'd won before I started working with him," Shilton points out, "was the Second and First Division Championships with Derby."

Shilton, though, is philosophical about Clough's attitude towards him publicly. "How many managers *will* say after a game: 'Oh, we'd have lost today but for our goalkeeper.' Goalkeeping is still looked upon as a negative role. I think managers are generally loathe to admit that their teams owe a lot to their goalkeepers. It seems, in some ways, a bad reflection on them."

Like a number of other players Shilton seemed to be going backwards prior to joining up with the remarkable Brian Clough/Peter Taylor partnership at Forest. His three years at Stoke had been something of a nightmare for him. He'd joined the club in 1974, desperate to achieve the success that had eluded him at Leicester. By the time he'd left in September 1977 Stoke were in the Second Division and Shilton, overshadowed by Ray Clemence in the England squad, had lost much of his charisma, despite his insistence that his overall form at Stoke had been good.

His loss of elevation in the game, together with the £300,000 transfer fee Stoke were asking for him, goes some way towards explaining why Stoke had to look long and hard for clubs willing to make a bid for Shilton. It hurt his pride considerably. "I couldn't accept that people were not willing to buy me ... surely, I felt, an agreement could be reached somewhere."

The fact that Clough and Taylor had faith in him, is something which Shilton finds impossible to overlook even today. "I don't forget anything in football, and I'll certainly never forget that Clough and Taylor not only had faith in me, but backed that faith. When things were going wrong at Stoke was when I wanted someone to come out and say: 'This boy can play ... he's a great goalkeeper,' but there was nobody doing that. Then Clough and Taylor signed me, and because I was playing in a successful team, people were saying: 'He's really playing well *now* ... he's *become* the best in the country.'"

Shilton likes to think that he and Clough are kindred spirits. He could always identify with Clough, long before the two started working together at Forest. Like Shilton the Forest manager had also gone through traumatic stages in his career when his individuality, outspokenness and hunger for success (following a playing career cruelly cut short by a broken leg) threatened to destroy him. And this was why, when Shilton's depression at Stoke was at its most intense, he immediately singled out Clough as a man who would appreciate how he felt and he arranged a meeting with Clough to discuss his problems.

"You always turn to people you think a lot of," Shilton says. "Brian Clough is my type of man. I don't agree with a lot of his methods and his attitudes to the game, but deep down I'm made the same way as he is in football terms."

The pair went for a meal together at a small guest house in Nottingham. "He just sat and listened to me," Shilton recalls. "He was obviously having to be careful about what he said, but he knew exactly how I felt and the way he handled it was incredible. I can't remember what I asked him, or what he said; it was all very general stuff. But the way he did it made a big impression on me. You know, it's the way people do things that matters, not necessarily what they do."

Clough and Shilton share a ruthless streak. Neither believes in going out of his way to win friends. Clough, a difficult man to understand and get to know intimately, has often admitted that. He doesn't mind whether players like him or not. "I'm not paid to be popular, that's not my job." It's the same with Shilton. "I can be a right pig," he says. "My missus says to me sometimes: 'Oh, where did you come from, you're not a bit like us.' She thinks I give off bad signals to people, although I don't try to. Sometimes I try to be ever so friendly and be totally in with them, but the next moment we're looking at each other and I'm not with them at all. My dad – now I call him a right silly so-and-so at times because I think he allows himself to be taken for a ride, but I know that if anything happened to him he'd never be short of friends."

Shilton is not as rude or dismissive of people as Clough can be but, says Shilton, "I know why he says the things he does to people. It's partly frustration and partly because when he sets his mind on something, he wants to achieve it so badly. I can appreciate that, because I want to succeed even more than he does."

In a way, these strong-willed characters give the impression of being rivals rather than colleagues. Such powerful personalities, one wonders whether Nottingham Forest is really big enough to accommodate the two of them. Not unnaturally, in view of his own background as one of Britain's most feared centre-forwards, Clough reacts strongly to suggestions that Shilton might have made a career for himself in that position.

(Clough's Derby once played Leicester in a testimonial match for Leicester defender Graham Cross and to add some interest to a low key game, Shilton came out of goal – he was replaced by Mark Wallington – and moved to the No. 9 role. The game changed completely with Shilton striving to show that he could be just as good as any outfield player and Derby's defenders, Roy McFarland and Colin Todd, then centre-back partners in the England team too, proving to be equally determined to avoid the ignominy of a goalkeeper getting the better of them. Shilton didn't score. But he came very close to it.)

"Oh no," Clough says, in one of those curiously cantankerous moods. "I'll tell you something . . . I've never spoken to him about this, but I bet that if given the choice he'd have wanted to be a centre-forward just as I really wanted to be a cricketer when I was a lad. He's sometimes played at centre-forward in training and he's hopeless – he wouldn't have made a No. 9 as long as pigeons flew!"

When discussing Brian Clough and Peter Taylor it's difficult for Shilton to separate the two. They

complement each other perfectly and, as seen in the problems they encountered when they were apart, at Leeds and Brighton, are at their most effective when working together. Clough has been described as a manager who "rules by fear", a reference to the fact that his ability to motivate teams is based on them directing most of the aggression he provokes into their performances.

Clough is a practitioner of the put-down. All his players must learn to eat humble pie. When Peter Withe scored four goals in a game, and asked whether he could be allowed to keep the match ball as a souvenir, Clough said curtly: "When you learn to play football I'll give you as many balls as you want." When Trevor Francis joined Forest in Britain's first £1 million transfer deal, someone from the Press asked Francis when he expected to make his debut. Before the striker could answer,

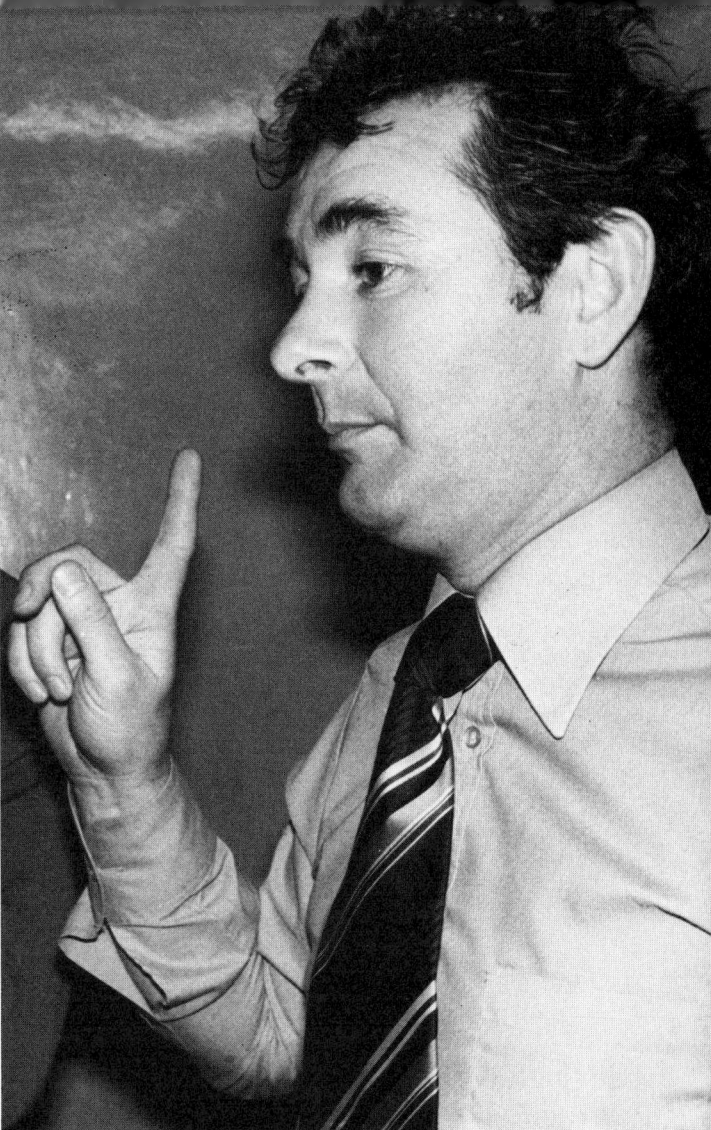

Shilton and Brian Clough . . . kindred spirits, but two powerful personalities whose relationship is potentially explosive. Clough on Shilton: "Never mind about what he has done for us – I've saved his career." Shilton on Clough: "All he'd won before I started working with him was the Second and First Division Championships with Derby County."

Clough put in his own blunt reply: "When I pick him." His authority at Forest is total and unsurpassed and he will fine players for breaches of club discipline in such an arbitrary manner it would bring about a union walk-out if adopted in any factory in the land.

Shilton once experienced Clough's verbally abrasive approach to the job when, after a 4–1 defeat by Derby, Clough reportedly said: "Shilton's money bags must be weighing him down." Shilton challenged Clough about that. "I objected not so much to the criticism, but the way it was given," he says. "Actually, when I went to see him, he claimed what he said had been taken out of context."

It's possible that such brushes between Clough and his players would be much more commonplace but for the presence of Taylor, who apart from being possibly the more knowledgeable of the two in terms of assessing players' strengths and weaknesses, and the finer points of the game, acts as a sort of dressing room diplomat. Taylor, an exceptionally humorous man, seems to have a restraining influence on Clough, as did Joe Mercer on Malcolm Allison when they were together at Manchester City. He helps smooth out the resentment created by Clough's acid tongue.

Taylor, a goalkeeper with Middlesbrough when Clough was a centre-forward there, has been prone to be protective of Shilton. "I've got a great feeling for goalkeepers and strikers," he says, admitting that if Shilton had a bad match and Clough criticised him for it he would be liable to counter-balance that by going up to him and "putting my arm around his shoulders . . . I shouldn't do it, but I do."

Taylor is, in fact, more generous in his praise of Shilton's contribution to Forest than Clough. When pressed, Clough says that "Shilton has played as big a part in our success as anyone." Taylor takes it a step further: "There are some players who win you matches and others who help win you matches. Peter wins you matches."

Taylor, who has the major responsibility at Forest for finding top-class players, has been a great admirer of Shilton since the latter's early days at Leicester, so much so that whenever he watched Leicester he'd focus his attention on Shilton rather than the game. "Goalkeepers come later than outfield players," he says. "You don't often get good teenage 'keepers but Shilton was one of the exceptions. He could do things at 18 or 19 that I could never do. I was totally obsessed with him." Taylor says that he became so fed up with listing Shilton's many strengths that he turned his attention towards his weaknesses. "Even then, I could only find one aspect of his game in which he wasn't better than our 'keeper at Derby, Les Green, and that was in his distribution of the ball."

"I didn't realise that I took so long to throw the ball out," Shilton says. "I always used to have to have a couple of looks around, you know, to see who best to give the ball to. Brian Clough and Peter Taylor used to point this out, jokingly really, but eventually it got through to me. This side of my game has come on unbelievably since at Forest."

Clough and Taylor tried to sign Shilton when they were at Derby. Taylor says that they made a £175,000 offer for him in writing ("That was the equivalent of three quarters of a million pounds today") and later, when Clough was at Leeds United (and Taylor at Brighton), Clough attempted to set up a part-exchange deal for Shilton, involving David Harvey and Joe Jordan or Gordon McQueen. The idea fell through due to Clough getting the sack after only 44 days at Elland Road.

On the day Forest signed Shilton, Taylor was so elated that he took him back to his house like a personal trophy. "He's the only player who's ever been to my home," Taylor says. "He told me he was going to look for a house, so I took him to mine to show him the district and the sort of properties . . . well, that was the excuse!"

Getting Shilton to sign on the dotted line had been a hard, often harrowing experience. Their initial meeting with Shilton to discuss his personal terms lasted more than three hours, punctuated by repeated signs of irritation from Clough, mostly in the form of him beating his squash racket against his legs. It culminated in Clough storming out of the meeting at 10.45 pm, followed by Taylor. "I'm going for a bloody meal," he said, leaving Shilton and his adviser Jon Holmes sitting in his City Ground office. Clough had originally offered Shilton £15,000 a year. It was agreed it could be pushed up to £17,000, but Shilton continued to hold out for the £22,000 he'd been getting at Stoke.

Shilton tied to break the deadlock by asking Stoke to pay a £5,000 loyalty bonus, due at the end of his contract with them, the reasoning being that they would be getting a good deal by selling him to Forest. Stoke refused ("It's the most incredible financial demand I've ever experienced," said chairman Albert Henshall) but when Clough, Taylor and Shilton got together again, they were able to reach a compromise figure of £20,000 a year. "I think they'd have paid anything to get me," Shilton maintains, "but at the end of the day, the money didn't really matter to me. I wanted to go there."

Despite such battles with Shilton, Clough says he likes as well as respects him. But he has had his patience tested. Towards the end of the 1980/81 season, for example, Shilton asked for a transfer on the grounds that he'd reached a stage in his career when he needed the fresh challenge of performing for a club on the continent. Seemingly to help this process, Shilton informed a Leicester freelance journalist of his intentions, getting him to release the story to the media so that it would be published and broadcast on Monday, 13th April.

It appeared a futile action to those close to Shilton because it was seemingly unthinkable that Clough and Taylor would allow such an important player to go. There had been a number of team changes at Forest that season and even Clough had publicly said that Shilton and striker Trevor Francis were the only members of the Forest first team squad whose places were secure. But Shilton reasoned that his transfer request might just work on the basis that Forest had been financially embarrassed by their failure to win a competition and even to get a place in the money-spinning UEFA Cup for the following season. Moreover, his contract was due to expire in 1982 and he was quick to point out to Forest that, under the new freedom-of-contract regulations, he would automatically become a free agent then. In those circumstances, Forest wouldn't get a transfer fee for him.

Shilton was proved right. On Thursday, 16th April, Clough and Taylor, much to the surprise of the general public and no doubt Shilton's fellow professionals, informed him that they were prepared to let him go, subject to them getting a "reasonable" fee and an adequate replacement being found for him.

Shilton was bothered, however, by the possibility that Clough and Taylor weren't serious, that they were merely using the situation to show their strength and get it across to Shilton that he wasn't indispensable. He was even more concerned about Taylor stressing to him that the club would make the appropriate announcement the following day and he should not make any comment about it publicly until after Forest's statement had been released. Shilton pondered the instruction from Taylor for some time, looking for reasons for it that possibly weren't there, and it occurred to him that if Taylor did release the news the following day it would appear in the national newspapers on Saturday morning. This was the day of Forest's League match at Aston Villa and Shilton didn't relish the prospect of having to appear in such an important game (Villa were contenders for the Championship) under such "unnecessary pressure".

So Shilton, a man not prepared to let anything or anyone get the upper hand on him, leaked yet another story to his journalist friend on Thursday night, much to Taylor's annoyance. It said that Forest were willing to let him go.

Shilton has become more relaxed since his days at Leicester and Stoke. It is an inevitable end-product of being in a successful team and the methods that Clough and Taylor employ to bring out the best in their men. But Shilton is still more intense than the Forest bosses would prefer.

The former Leicester manager Jimmy Bloomfield could never understand Shilton's intensity. "He likes to do certain things all the time and he didn't feel so good if he didn't," he recalls. "I didn't think that a lot of those things were necessary . . . he should have had more confidence in his own ability. All right, he could do them if he wanted, but if he couldn't because of injury or whatever, it shouldn't have mattered to him as much as it did."

Clough agrees: "There are people in the game who have had to work just as hard, if not harder than Peter, but that's because they haven't had his ability. In other words, I don't think Peter has

needed to put as much thought and effort into it. I mean, it's much easier for Frank Sinatra to sing than somebody who can't sing. Obviously to stay at the top, Sinatra has had to do this, he's had to do that, but he's led a hell of a life Sinatra has when you analyse it and yet his voice at 65 has stood the test of time better than anyone else's."

Clough insists that, in terms of Shilton's mental approach, he's helped him more than all his previous managers put together. "You'd be staggered at how much help even the best footballers need," he says. "They need *more* help than the ordinary ones sometimes, because they've got more to lose. They're so insecure sometimes it's incredible."

Peter Taylor occasionally tried to "release" Shilton from his search for perfection by trying to engage him in conversation about it.

"Don't you think you overdo it?" Taylor once asked Shilton.

"No, I don't think so . . ."

"Well, I think you do . . . I think you're obsessed."

"I tried to tell him to moderate it," Taylor says now, "but it's very difficult to tell someone like him to put the brake on slightly."

Not surprisingly, Clough is rather more forceful. "On a few occasions I've said to Peter after a training session: 'Come on, Peter, get in the bath.' He's looked at me as if to say he's wanted to do a bit more. 'Peter, get in that bath!'"

Shilton smiles at the memory, but shakes his head emphatically when you suggest that Clough forced him to ease up. "Brian Clough and Peter Taylor haven't forced me to do anything," he says, knowing that it's not strictly true.

Shilton says: "I've always been a team man, very much so, but goalkeeping is an individual position. And I've always been a loner, a little bit moody, especially in the terms of the training I've wanted to do. For example, when I was at Leicester, I didn't think that all the running the other players did was any good for me, and all the managers and coaches left me to do whatever I wanted – no, the one exception was Willie Bell, who was Leicester's caretaker manager for a while. He insisted that I train with the rest of the team and that was right. You have to be part of the team, the set-up, and this is what happens at Forest. I do the same training as the other players, although I'm obviously allowed a little leeway and anything outside that I have to fit in during my spare time."

One of the great things about being at Forest, Shilton says, is that Clough and Taylor encourage the players to use their own initiative. All the players do the same basic training and are then left to their own devices, to do the specific work relevant to their individual positions or roles.

It's a situation Shilton welcomes. "Somebody isn't coming up to you and saying : 'I want you to do this' or 'I want you to do that' all the time. A lot of managers and coaches do the thinking for the players and really the players can get very lazy. They've got to use their own initiative, because when you're out on that pitch in a match, no-one can tell you what to do then."

But even Shilton's resourcefulness was stretched to the limit during Forest's preparations for the 1980 European Cup Final against West Germany's Hamburg in Madrid.

Forest's 1–0 win was highlighted by a Shilton performance which must rank as one of the most inspired goalkeeping displays ever seen in the competition. The background to the succession of magnificent saves Shilton made on that famous night provides an insight into the extraordinary relationship between the goalkeeper and his manager. It is why Shilton sometimes refers to Clough and Taylor as geniuses.

Ten days before the final Clough took his first team squad away for a week's break at Calla Millor in Majorca. The aim was to brush the tension out of the team following a gruelling season in which they'd taken part in more than 80 matches, to get them in the right frame of mind for their three-day build-up for the last – and most important – battle against Hamburg.

The idea created problems for Shilton, because "my sharpness comes from what I do in training rather than in matches" and he had his doubts that the facilities where he was due to stay in Majorca would be ideal for the training he felt he needed. His fears were justified. There wasn't a grass pitch where Forest were staying and he had to improvise on sand, and on a small grass verge just outside Forest's hotel. He'd become almost neurotic about all this by the time Forest arrived in Madrid on the Monday night, two days before the match.

"That night", Shilton recalls, "I kept nagging Brian Clough and Peter Taylor. 'When are we going to train?' and 'Is there a grass pitch there?' I kept asking. We were staying right up in the mountains and I'd been told that there was a grass pitch alongside the all-weather pitch we were going to use for our preparations. But when we got there on Tuesday, lo and behold, no grass pitch! It was so funny. The night before the European Cup Final I'm looking for a piece of grass only as big as your

front lawn. I'd have given £1,000 for it."

Shilton eventually found, and had to make do with, a piece of turf no more than 10-yards square adjoining the all-weather pitch. He also found a traffic island with "trees and bits of grass" on it, but his attempts to use it for training were foiled by men working on the road.

Clough grins at the memory. "Oh, he told you what we did to him in Madrid did he? It was the best help we could have given him . . . it removed him from himself. He was always on about grass, grass, grass . . . chuntering on he was. Still, rabbiting on about me at least took his mind off Hamburg."

According to Shilton, Clough is unerringly brilliant at saying the right things at the right times to his players. On the eve of the final, for example, Clough called him back as the players stepped off the coach for a training session and related a conversation he'd had earlier with a newspaper reporter. "You know, I can't believe it," Clough said, "this reporter has just said to me: 'Don't you think Hamburg have the edge now that you have lost Trevor Francis (he missed the Hamburg game through injury) and they have Kevin Keegan?' You know what I told him? 'Well, we've got the better goalkeeper than them, we've got the best goalkeeper in the world, so isn't that just as big an advantage as them having Keegan.'"

During Forest's team meetings, Clough often used Keegan as a catalyst to stimulate his players, perhaps Shilton especially. Not long previously, Keegan had irritated Shilton by stating that he considered his ex-Liverpool colleague, Ray Clemence, the better 'keeper, suggesting that Shilton was more flamboyant but less effective. Clough referred to that during his eve-of-the-match tactical briefing: "You lads don't have to worry about Keegan . . . as soon as he comes into our box, Peter Shilton will knock his block off."

Peter Taylor, Shilton says, also deserves full marks as a psychologist. On the eve of the game, when Shilton was concerned about having pulled a calf muscle in his left leg in training earlier that day (an injury which was to require three pain-killing injections before the kick-off), Taylor dominated the stage with an act which any stand-up comic would have been proud of. "It was too early to go to bed when we got back from training," Shilton recalls. "There was no TV in our rooms, no anything, and all we could have done was to sit down and talk about the game, which in itself would have created tension, especially among the younger players. All of a sudden, as we were sitting outside

the hotel having a few drinks, Peter Taylor comes up and asks Garry Birtles (a player with a penchant for trendy scruffiness) to bring down his radio. For the next hour, he went on and on about this radio, cracking jokes about it – you know: 'This radio is filthy – has it been kept in a coalhouse', things like that, and it was so funny it was like a cabaret. It was sheer brilliance in my opinion that he could talk for an hour about it and keep everyone interested.''

But it is Clough's role as an antagonist that has really stood Forest – and Shilton – in good stead in their successful battles for the major prizes. On the day of the Hamburg game, when the Forest players were sitting with him on their hotel verandah, Clough asked defender Ken Burns: ''Ken, do you know what we've got to do tonight?''

''Yes, I think ...'' Before Burns could finish the sentence, Clough repeated the question, this time

Peter Taylor, Clough's right-hand man, who helps ease the dressing-room resentment created by his partner's abrasiveness. A former goalkeeper himself, Taylor admits that he idolises Shilton. "There are some players who win you matches and others who help win you matches. Peter Shilton wins you matches."

more forcibly. ''Don't bloody think ... do you *know* what you've got to do?''

Clough then heard a voice from behind him mutter testily: ''We all know what we've got to do. ****ing shut up!''

''That's the state the lads were in after 10 days in my company,'' Clough says proudly. ''We could have taken on two German teams that night, not one.''

Shilton has generally enjoyed playing for Clough and Taylor because ''everything is right, everything is honest. Nobody gets away with anything and

when we get out on the pitch, all 11 players know what they've got to do. It's like any job . . . you have a basic responsibility to the fellow next to you.

"I feel I'm on the same wavelength as them and vice versa," Shilton says. "Previously, if I saw something going wrong at a club I had to say or do something about it – I didn't want to, because there are enough pressures in my job as it is, but you see I couldn't always count on the man at the top doing it. That's not been the case at Forest, because I've known the boss and I have been thinking along the same lines.

"I think I've always needed pretty strong handling . . . I've always needed someone there who could say: 'Look, I'm the boss'. Brian Clough and Peter Taylor used to pull my leg about it when I first came to Forest . . . in front of all the other players, one of them would say: 'He ran the team meetings at Leicester and Stoke but he doesn't do it any more.' Things like that. They were right.

"In a team who aren't functioning right because certain players aren't doing their jobs properly, that's when you look for honesty, not so much from the men around you, but from the manager and the coach. This is where Brian Clough is so good . . . he recognises every aspect of every position on the field and usually I can count on total honesty from him. If we get beaten 5–0 and I know I've done everything right, I can rely on him to pinpoint exactly what went wrong in the team.

"Up to joining Forest, I'd had a lot of disappointments in my career, and yes, it was partly my fault. Then all of a sudden I found exactly what I wanted ... I found honesty, I found strength and I found brilliance. For the first time in my career I was contented.

"Brian Clough and Peter Taylor have obviously motivated me up to a point, but one thing I want to make clear is that I've generally produced superb performances for England during my four years at Forest and there has been no motivation on the part of Brian Clough and Peter Taylor on those occasions. The difference between me now and when I was at Leicester and Stoke, is that I've got a successful and consistent team in front of me. I think it's important to be with a club like that if you're an international

because you don't get quite so up-tight about the so-called big games – every match you play is a big game – and you are always in the limelight.

"Not only this, I've matured as I've grown older. I know myself better; I know how I feel, how I think and what I can do."

Apart from Clough and Taylor, another man who can be said to have figured prominently in Shilton's success story at Nottingham Forest is an extraordinary character by the name of Len Heppell, a 62-year-old former English national professional ballroom champion – and in more recent years a nightclub owner – from Hexham, County Durham. Heppell has made a name for himself as an expert on body movement, rhythm and balance in relation to sport and first met Shilton when Don Revie, then England manager, invited him to the international squad's training headquarters in Hertfordshire, to give the players the opportunity of hearing his gospel. ("Seventy per cent of professional footballers could improve if they were taught rhythm and balance," is the message on the front of Heppell's promotional pamphlet.)

At that time, Shilton felt there was something in his game that wasn't right, but couldn't put his finger on it. Heppell did – he told Shilton that he didn't stand or move properly and the ensuing advice gave Shilton the "completeness" for which he'd been looking for as long as he could remember. "It gave me that extra dimension to my game," he says.

But first, who's this man Len Heppell? In his promotional pamphlet it states that "originally tone deaf and lacking an inborn sense of rhythm, he taught himself to dance and six years later became a ballroom champion." Heppell was 25 at the time, working as a garage mechanic. Sports-mad, he took up cricket at 34, golf at 36, table tennis at 41, squash at 57, and helped by the body rhythm lessons he later imparted to others, quickly reached a high standard in all these sports. "I'm my best advert," he says.

Among his earliest pupils was his daughter, Maureen, who "despite lacking natural ball sense and rhythm" achieved national table tennis honours within three years of her starting in the game, and an all-time English record of winning 14 open tournaments out of a possible 17 (she was runner-up in the other three). Heppell's sister, like his daughter, was an international table tennis player and he himself was good enough at the game to reach the county seedings and win the Scottish open championship at 49. "I played Kevin Keegan at

---

The part Shilton played in Nottingham Forest's Championship triumph in 1978 is spotlighted by his mood of defiance in their match at Coventry. Forest needed a point to clinch the title and not surprisingly in view of Shilton's presence, they got it with a 0–0 draw. It was Shilton's 22nd "clean sheet" in 32 Championship matches.

midnight once," he recalls, "gave him a 10 start and still beat him. Hammered him."

He also helped transform the career of his son-in-law Bryan "Pop" Robson, the former Sunderland and West Ham striker. At the start of his career, at Newcastle, Robson was considered too slow to be an outstanding striker and was thinking about quitting the game to become a professional golfer. "I felt embarrassed for him when I watched him play because he was so slow over the first few yards," Heppell says. "'Well, Bryan,' I told him, 'if that's all you're lacking I can make you quick.'" Robson's problem, Heppell says, is that he wasn't "leading" with his head ("the heaviest part of your body") when turning and running. The pair worked on it during the summer and the following season Robson, whose previous highest total of goals in a season had been just 6, got around 30. "Jackie Milburn (the former Newcastle and England centre-forward) asked me: 'What's happened to Pop? He's like a sprinter with lead taken out of his boots.'"

Despite his age, Heppell himself is no slouch when it comes to being able to react quickly to a situation. A frail-looking, ferret-like figure (he stands just 5 ft. 5 in. and weighs 9½ stone), he runs on nervous energy. "You see the way I'm sitting in this chair," he says. "I'm sitting like Kevin Keegan does . . . if he sits down it's on the edge of the chair. I never relax – I've got to think to relax. People can do what I do but they're lazy. It's hard work always being aware and sharp. You've got to think sharpness. I've worked at it."

Football professionals are notoriously suspicious of outsiders but Heppell, who talks as quickly as he moves and oozes a boyish Geordie charm, has been able to pierce the barrier better than most. He certainly made a big impact on Shilton, not to mention a number of other England players. He has continued to keep in touch with the England squad from time to time under Ron Greenwood's management, and has worked with a number of English League players and clubs, not to mention professionals in other sports such as boxing and lawn tennis.

Heppell had wanted to meet Shilton since watching him beaten by a low shot in Poland's 1–1 draw with England in a World Cup qualifying tie at Wembley in October 1973, a result which enabled the Poles to clinch a place, at England's expense, in the final stages of the competition in West Germany the following year. It had seemed to Heppell that Shilton had gone down a fraction too late for the ball, and as he says: "I couldn't wait to get my hands on him."

When Revie invited Heppell to the England training session, Heppell recalls that Shilton was the first player to take an interest in what he had to offer. "He's like other great players, like Alan Ball and Bobby Moore," Heppell says. "They want to jump on because they don't want to miss anything."

"Peter asked us to watch him from behind the goal, and then he said: 'What do you think?' I said, 'Peter, can I speak the truth?' He wanted me to tell him, so that gave me the confidence to speak up you see. I said: 'Peter, you're too stiff.' Fancy me coming out with that to Peter Shilton!

"Peter had worked a lot on weight training. He looked too big and strong to be agile."

According to Heppell, Shilton had been jumping up and down when the ball was being played around his penalty area by the Poles at Wembley and was off his feet in the split second that Anton Domarski hit the decisive shot. One of Shilton's problems, Heppell reasoned, was that his stance was too upright. Also, his body was like a huge coil spring. "You know, the big coil spring that you get in your car. Really big and heavy, with little bend or suppleness in it." What was needed, he decided, was for Shilton to practise moving around as if "part of that spring had been taken away and replaced by hundreds and hundreds of little watch springs." When they went for walks around the hotel, Heppell advised him to try and be "like an object which can be seen shimmering through a heat haze." Later, Shilton spent some time practising the technique alone in his local park, "exaggerating it until it became a habit and not so much of a conscious effort."

Heppell, who feels that Shilton's resulting greater suppleness has also caused him to become better equipped to hold shots as opposed to stopping them, beams with pride when he watches him in action today. "He's like Bjorn Borg. The difference between Borg and Jimmy Connors is that Connors has to train all the time to move well because he moves with strength and when he loses that his game is off. But Borg is like a big cat isn't he? It's the same with Shilton. When Shilton is strolling about his penalty area you can see a lot of Borg in him."

Jubilant scenes at Coventry. Shilton and Forest defender Kenny Burns give vent to their emotions, as does one of the Forest fans who ran onto the pitch at the end to join in their team's celebrations. "I think this picture shows the tremendous bond between players in a good team," Shilton says, "It's not a bond of friendship – it's asking the impossible for everyone to like each other – but one of respect."

4

MAGIC
IN THE MOUTH

Shilton, on the trampoline, developing his "unbeatable" image.

"There is more to goalkeeping than just keeping goal," Peter Shilton is fond of saying. His definition of the perfect goalkeeper: one who never needs to make a save.

Through his stature in the game, personality, presence and ability to organise the men immediately in front of him a goalkeeper can not only help prevent dangerous situations developing but himself being forced into action. Shilton looks upon this as one of his hidden strengths. It's a sore point, moreover, with him that it tends to be overlooked "even by so-called good judges of football"; that he, and other goalkeepers, are too often judged on the basis of their physical contribution to a match.

Other goalkeepers, and those outfield defenders who have played with him, certainly appreciate Shilton's expertise in this area. Mark Wallington, whose willingness to take on the responsibility of giving his team-mates instructions and the occasional motivation-boost, led to him being appointed Leicester's captain, says this is the part of Shilton's game that excites him the most ("He's like the conductor of an orchestra"). Larry Lloyd, the centre-half in front of Shilton during Nottingham Forest's tremendous run of success, regularly made a point of turning around to face Shilton a second or two before the start of a match to make a "talking" gesture with his hands so as to reiterate how much he relied upon the 'keeper's vociferous approach.

"He went over the top occasionally," Lloyd says. "Kenny Burns (Lloyd's centre-back partner at Forest) and I had a lot of arguments with "Shilts". But arguments or not, I still preferred him to make the noise he did during a match, than having someone behind me not making any noise at all. I'm sure most other centre-halves would say the same."

Brian Clough and Peter Taylor also appreciate this side of Shilton's game. "It's one of the reasons why I've enjoyed playing for them so much," Shilton says. "They are dynamic people who realise how much influence footballers like that can have on a team. And that in itself, has given me a lot of confidence."

But it still rankles that his ability to "read" situations and his personality – "two of my biggest strengths" – are not appreciated more widely. "People completely dismiss them," he says. "They see the shots I save, the crosses I take and what have you, but they don't see the confidence, determination and discipline I can instil into a team by shouting the right things at the right time. It's *got* to be done. This sort of responsibility should be shared, but the man at the back – the last line of defence – should still be the dominant one. All the play is in front of him and he can see so much more than the other players.

"The people in front of you are not dummies and it's amazing how much you can pull out of them. I've had some magnificent matches in this respect, but I pick up the newspapers the next day and I read: 'Peter Shilton had nothing to do', or somebody says to me: 'Easy day yesterday, Peter.' It's so frustrating because I *know* that's not been the case."

All of which explains why, when Shilton is asked to name what he considers his best performances, he doesn't automatically single out his display in the 1980 European Cup Final against Hamburg, or any other matches in which the amount of physical work he's had to do has almost created the impression of him playing the opposition virtually on his own.

For example, Shilton's eyes immediately light up when he discusses a Nottingham Forest pre-season friendly match against a Norwegian amateur team at Haelstrom in Norway in August 1979, when the opposition were more than a little surprised – and inspired – by having Shilton on their side for the second half.

"The first 45 minutes were a bit embarrassing really," Shilton recalls, "because we were 4–0 up and it could easily have been 10." At half-time Shilton was told by Clough to go into the Norwegian team's goal for the rest of the match. It was an instruction which Shilton suspects had something to do with the fact that he'd been involved in long, arduous negotiations with the manager over a new contract. He interpreted it as Clough's way of trying to pull him down a peg or two. "I think he felt that the lads would help him get one over on me by taking the micky," Shilton says.

If that was the case, then the plan misfired badly. Shilton is never more effective than when he's in one of his hyper-aggressive, defiant moods and on that particular day, his determination to get back at Clough quickly spread to his new teammates. "I got them all out onto the pitch a couple of minutes before the re-start," Shilton says, "and I just put my fist up to them and kept saying: 'No goals' ... 'no goals'...." Most of them couldn't speak English, but they all must have got the message after five minutes when Shilton and Forest's England striker Tony Woodcock challenged each other for a 50-50 through ball. "Tony got there a fraction of a second before me," Shilton recalls, "and I just came roaring in behind him and nearly knocked his head off. He didn't half give me a dirty look." Shilton hardly ever stopped shouting during those 45 minutes and, despite the language barrier, was able to get enough basic instructions across to his defenders to make life more than a little difficult for their high-priced English League opponents.

Much to Forest's embarrassment, the match eventually ended 5–1 and the only time Shilton was really called upon to keep the ball out of the net himself was when John Robertson scored Forest's only goal of the half – from a penalty. "Forest's dressing room was quiet after the match," Shilton says, "and that was the best possible compliment I've ever had in my life."

Other performances in that category include the second leg of Forest's European Cup semi-final against Holland's Ajax in 1980. Forest, under pressure for most of the match, restricted Ajax to only a handful of scoring chances and, despite the 1–0 defeat, went through 2–1 on aggregate; it was regarded as one of their best defensive performances since their return to the First Division three years previously. Shilton likes to think that despite his comparative inactivity, physically, he deserved as much credit as the other defenders because of his "concentration and involvement in the game" for the full 90 minutes. "It was incredible," he says. "The sweat was pouring from me when I came off that field. I was shattered."

Shilton is exhausted, mentally as well as physically, after every match. There is, he points out, a very thin line between being sufficiently involved in a match to help the men around him, and too involved. "I've talked to John Burridge (Queen's Park Rangers' goalkeeper) a hell of a lot about this," Shilton says. "There was a tendency for him to get too involved. There could have been a stage in the season when he might have cracked because he couldn't possibly take all the mental and physical pressure he puts on himself. I think he's now got the right balance, just as I have.

"In some matches, I'll be shouting my head off all the time," he adds, "but in others I'll be fairly quiet. It just depends how the game's going."

He underlined the point by recalling England's 2–0 win over Spain in Barcelona in March 1980. England had been well on top for much of the match, but began to ease up 15 to 20 minutes from the end and allow the Spaniards to come strongly into the picture for the first time. "We could easily have let it go," Shilton says. "We'd only relaxed slightly but I thought: 'Hell, if they get a goal now, there's a good chance of them sticking two or three in.' From that point on I started shouting non-stop and I could see the lads responding. Suddenly we really tightened up and killed the Spaniards off. They were gone after 10 minutes."

It can work the other way around sometimes, with other players shouting at Shilton, although it's very rare to see one of his defenders remonstrating with him as right-back Viv Anderson did in the European Cup Final against Hamburg. There had been a misunderstanding between them, resulting in Anderson needing to perform a minor miracle to clear a ball, which he felt Shilton should have gone for. The TV cameras focused on Anderson screaming and gesticulating at the 'keeper as if it was a football moment to be recorded for posterity and Shilton raised an arm to acknowledge the validity of Anderson's criticism. "I welcomed it," Shilton says. "I'm no different to anyone else ... even I need a good ear-bashing from time to time."

It seems strange that Shilton should attach so much importance to his role as a motivator and organiser because at Forest he has played with one of the best back-fours in the country. Viv Anderson, Larry Lloyd, Ken Burns and Frank Gray, Forest's defenders in the European Cup Final, have all played at international level. Lloyd and Burns, the centre-backs and thus the players who come into contact with Shilton the most, were among the most experienced professionals in the First Division. But would Lloyd and Burns have been so good had they not had Shilton behind them?

Shilton is flattered by the picture of him as a man who pulls the string like a puppet master and helps turn good centre-backs into great ones but is inevitably embarrassed when you put that analogy to him in relation to the influence he had on Lloyd and Burns. "I can't say I made them good players because I rely on my defenders as much as they do on me," he says. "It's a two-way thing. Larry Lloyd and Ken Burns helped me because, in addition to their basic technical ability, they are both extremely positive. It was easy for me to read what they were going to do in certain situations and, if necessary, tie up all the loose ends. There's nothing worse for a 'keeper than having defenders who aren't decisive, who want to stand off opponents and let things happen."

In this respect, Shilton cites the case of Ipswich's Paul Cooper, who was widely described as one of the most improved goalkeepers in England during the 1980/81 season, in which Ipswich came close to achieving the Championship-FA Cup-UEFA Cup treble. Shilton feels that Cooper has benefited enormously through the emergence of young centre-backs Russell Osman and Terry Butcher as regular members of the Ipswich team, "if only because of their decisiveness."

"I take on a lot of responsibility and I expect the defenders in front of me to do the same," Shilton says. "When you have a goalkeeper like me, I think there is a danger occasionally of defenders relying too much on him. For example, if there's a high ball in the box they'll perhaps think: 'Oh, I won't go for that, let the 'keeper get it' when really they should be taking the initiative themselves. I don't work that way ... I work on honesty and on people doing their jobs and, in a sense, that means getting it across to my defenders that I'm not perfect. Sometimes two of us will be going for the same ball, which will mean me having to clatter the other bloke to the ground or him clattering me. But at least one of us will get that ball.

"When you talk about me organising Larry Lloyd and Ken Burns ... well, I suppose I did up to a point, but I'd prefer to say that I advised and helped them. Footballers are only human and Larry and Kenny, being a bit fiery, could have a 10–15 minute spell in the match when their concentration wasn't right, when they weren't quite clicking. I'd be right on their backs and, even though they were liable to look at me as if to say 'shut up' I wouldn't until they'd got through it.

"I never got any real aggro from them because they accepted it was part of my job."

Lloyd nods in agreement. He has always looked upon himself as a positive player, but adds that this was particularly the case when he was operating in front of Peter Shilton and Ray Clemence at Nottingham Forest and Liverpool. "If there's a man behind you by the name of Shilton or Clemence – any good goalkeeper for that matter – then it gives you that extra bit of confidence to go for the ball," Lloyd says. "If it's a dodgy goalkeeper, you're almost afraid to commit yourself for fear that, if you miss the tackle or anything like that, the ball will end up in the net."

One of the great advantages of having a Peter Shilton is that such men, through having created an aura of invincibility, are inclined to lift teammates merely by their presence ... and at the same time deflate those opposing them.

During Leicester City training sessions Shilton preferred to face shots from the apprentice professionals rather than his first-team colleagues because the latter group, seemingly anxious to keep their self-confidence intact, tended not to take "shooting" seriously. "Peter used the apprentices because they were afraid to take the micky out of him," Mark

Wallington says. "The first-team lads would attempt to do all kinds of things with the ball, but as Peter often told them: 'You wouldn't try these shots against me in a competitive match because you wouldn't have the time ... and you wouldn't have the bottle.'"

Forest's men, too, appreciate the psychological problems involved in getting the ball past Shilton. "I get the feeling that they're conscious of my reputation and determination when hitting shots at me in training. They try and hit the perfect ball all the time and don't give themselves any margin for error. This sounds a little conceited, I know, but I'm sure that against a lot of other goalkeepers, they'd just hit it without thinking quite so much about it."

Even highly accomplished and experienced teams, such as Liverpool, can be "psyched" by Shilton. In recent seasons, no side have had a better record against Bob Paisley's machine-like Liverpool team than Nottingham Forest. They met them 14 times between 1977/78 (Forest's first season back in Division One) and 1980/81 ... and lost only twice. Forest conceded no more than six goals in those matches, and among their most notable successes were their victories over Liverpool in the 1978 League Cup Final (which Shilton missed as he was ineligible), 1979 European Cup first round and 1980 League Cup semi-finals.

In some of the matches, Shilton noted a distinct lack of confidence in Liverpool's finishing. "I'm not saying it was me," he says, "but it was incredible the way they'd get into good shooting positions and then, instead of attempting to score from there, try and work the ball into an even better position."

Shilton, ironically, has long insisted that a high number of teams contribute to their downfall against Liverpool through being "frightened" of their reputation. He remembers particularly a clear-cut scoring chance created for their centre-forward David Johnson, in the second leg of the 1979/80 League Cup semi-final at Anfield. Johnson was unmarked on the edge of Shilton's six-yards box when the ball was pulled back for him from the goal-line and, as Shilton observed, all he really needed to do to find the net was get his head to it. "But Johnson tried to direct the ball just inside the post, to make doubly sure that I couldn't get to it, and it went wide."

Although Shilton insists that he treats every match the same, in terms of his determination to keep a clean sheet, it's fair to say that he derives a particular satisfaction in doing that at Liverpool's

Kenny Burns (left) and Larry Lloyd (above), two defenders who benefited most from Shilton's dominating style. They, more than anyone, appreciated the confidence, determination and discipline he can bring to a team through his presence, stature and "shouting" on the field. "But," Shilton stresses, "men like Larry and Ken have helped me as much as I've helped them because they are extremely positive players and therefore make it easy for a goalkeeper to read what they are going to do."

Lloyd, he says, has never really been given the praise he deserves. "When he was in the First Division, people were inclined to look upon him as just a big stopper but there were times when he showed an incredibly delicate touch on the ball for someone of his build. He was great at chipping balls – when I faced him in training at Forest, he'd shape to blast the ball at me and then suddenly, without checking, sort of scoop the ball up so that it came at me like a nine-iron chip shot in golf. It was incredible the way he did it. Larry's greatest attribute was his ability to win the ball, especially in the air, but make no mistake, the man could play a bit."

---

expense. It stems not so much from the Nottingham Forest/Liverpool rivalry, but that which has existed even longer – between Shilton and Ray Clemence.

Shilton is the last professional footballer who would be expected to leave any stones unturned in his exploration of ways to gain an edge over opponents. The psychological aspect of goalkeeping, in particular, has been given a lot of thought. He makes a point, for instance, of sprinting onto the field and looking impressive during the pre-match warm-up period. "Some goalkeepers go out a bit casual and sloppy but that's something I never do," Shilton says. "Footballers do have a look around when they're kicking in. If they catch sight of an opposing goalkeeper who appears to be really sharp, well . . ."

Standing six feet Shilton is by no means the tallest goalkeeper in the English League – Manchester City's Joe Corrigan is 6 ft 4 in, for example, and West Ham's Phil Parkes 6 ft 2 in – but his 13 stone frame, embodying a $16\frac{1}{2}$ inch neck, 42 inch chest and 34 inch waist, is possibly the most intimidating and clearly packed with power. As a result, opposing forwards often "freeze" when running towards Shilton's goal with the ball.

Says Larry Lloyd, who at 6ft 2in and more than 12 stone is no midget either: "I've seen forwards get past me with all the confidence of a Pele or Johan Cruyff and then, faced by 'Shilts', suddenly lose their nerve. I mean, it's happened to me when I've tried to beat him in training. All he has to do is crouch a little bit, and he sort of spreads and fills the bloody goal up."

Little wonder that even ultra-aggressive forwards such as Joe Jordan, men for whom physical intimidation is an essential part of the game, are inclined to think twice before tangling with Shilton. He can recall only two who have been sufficiently courageous (or foolhardy) to try and mix it with him. One was former Middlesbrough centre-forward John Hickton: "He often came sliding in for through balls with his foot up." The other was Manchester City outside-right, Tommy Hutchison, when he was with Coventry: "He was always having a verbal dig at me."

Shilton has not only always set his sights on becoming better than other goalkeepers technically and mentally, but fitter and stronger too. Even today, after around 15 years at the top, he continues to look after his body in the hope that he can continue as an English League footballer until he's 40. In addition to his training, Shilton eats plenty of high-protein food ("I have meat nearly every day"), drinks a lot of milk, and ensures that he has an average of at least 10 hours sleep a night. "I can put on weight," says Shilton, "but it's only gradual and only up to a point of six pounds or so. In any case I can lose four pounds or more in one training session." His ideal weight is between 13 st. 7 lb. and 13 st. 10 lb. "If I go under 13 st. 7 lb. I don't feel strong."

After a training session it's not unusual for Shilton to drink a large pot of tea or coffee (he doesn't take sugar). And tea is all he has now for breakfast each morning. "It's amazing how your eating habits change as you get older," he says. "As a youngster my mother would make me this huge breakfast of eggs, bacon, sausages, toast – the lot. Even on the match days. But if you were to give me that today ... ugh!"

At the start of his career at Leicester Shilton exercised in his spare time, building up his strength with light weights and calisthenics. "I wanted to be able to stand up to the physical side of the game," he says. The reward of that work is the surprisingly low number of matches Shilton has missed through injury since making his English League debut around 700 competitive matches ago. "One can be unlucky with injuries, but there's no harm in taking precautions," he says. "Football's like everything else – it's all about percentages, and I think you've got to try and get every single percentage on your side."

Later in Shilton's career, after establishing himself as a regular member of Leicester's first team, his search for supreme fitness led him to a man by the name of Jock Scott. Scott was then a physical training instructor at a gymnasium in Loughbrough, and had been a *PTI* in the army for more than 25 years before that. Over a period of two years, Scott, a judo black belt, spent one morning a week with Shilton at a local army training camp, putting him through the punishing routines with which he'd "tortured" so many of the soldiers under his jurisdiction. One such routine entailed Shilton doing 15 to 20 exercises in quick succession, including weightlifting, rope-climbing, jumping with weights, with a sprint from one end of the large gym to the other in between each one. That was followed by gymnastic exercises on a trampoline to improve his reactions and agility.

"The other Leicester City players came down once but they didn't like it at all," Scott recalls. Neither did the Leicester Tigers Rugby Union team, who ended up "lying around being sick all over the place." Scott laughs when you suggest that they all might have looked upon him as a sadist. "Well, I suppose I am," he replies, almost proudly.

"I like doing things that are different," Shilton says. "And quite apart from the fact that the sort of training I did with Jock Scott was beneficial to me, physically, it was also good for my image. (It attracted considerable media attention and was featured in the Blue Peter children's programme on BBC TV.) I don't think Jock thought much of it initially ... I'm sure he looked upon it as no more than a publicity stunt and wanted to really make me suffer." But Scott soon changed his opinions about Shilton, and indeed professional footballers generally.

"He said he badly wanted to do it," Scott recalls, "so I decided to chase the backside off him, try and break him if you want to put it that way. When I was in the army, I had to force people to do things but Peter, well, he was top-of-the-class. There were times when I thought: 'Oh, he's going to sit down any moment now and say he's had enough', but he never did."

Shilton, through his voluntary extra training stints at a local army camp, was once featured in the Blue Peter BBC TV programme. Getting a lighthearted introduction to the assault course are the programme's presenters of the time, Peter Purves and John Noakes.

Shilton feels he's particularly strong in the stomach ("no-one has harder stomach muscles than me") and the wrists and hands. When Don Revie was England's manager, Shilton and the other members of the international squad were subjected to various physical tests, one of which was to measure the strength of their grips. Shilton recorded the highest pressure, and the grip in his right hand was exactly the same as in his left.

One of Shilton's close friends, Gravesend FC chairman Roger Easterby, once gave Shilton the name "Powerful Pierre" (a reference also to his Continental-like appearance) and the nickname was immediately coined by his wife Sue. When she answers the 'phone to a friend or member of the family, she'll often ask: "Do you want to talk to 'Powerful'?" At Leicester some of his teammates referred to him as "Tarzan".

Shilton, however, has not always found his he-man image beneficial.

The image was projected most forcibly when he was at Leicester and featured in an advertising campaign for the Bullworker body-building machine with other leading sportsmen such as Muhammad Ali. Shilton's endorsement of the machine ("In five easy minutes each day, you can begin to build the dynamic power-packed body you've always wanted" claimed one advert) must have made a considerable impact on his fans because, even today, supporters will often ask him: "How's that Bullworker?"

But the advertisement rebounded upon him when he was in the struggling Stoke City team. Some critics (including Sam Bartram, the former Charlton goalkeeper and now a football reporter with the Sunday People) suggested that he wasn't agile enough.

"I was supposed to be 'top-heavy', or 'muscle-bound'," Shilton says, getting visibly hot under the collar at the memory. "It was the biggest load of rubbish I've ever heard in my life." He suspects the Bullworker endorsement did much to create the impression of him being too muscular, as did the fact that he's so broad across the shoulders. "I *look* big, right? Gordon Banks looked big too, as he had heavy thighs. The people who claimed that I built up my body to look the way I do should meet my younger brother – he's built exactly the same way as me, only he's a bit fatter.

"People are always looking for ways to knock you when you're in unsuccessful teams," Shilton says. "However many good games you have, there'll always be people trying to pick out something bad.

"Too heavy? Muscle bound? You set up any exercise on agility with the big men in the game, and I'd be confident against any of them."

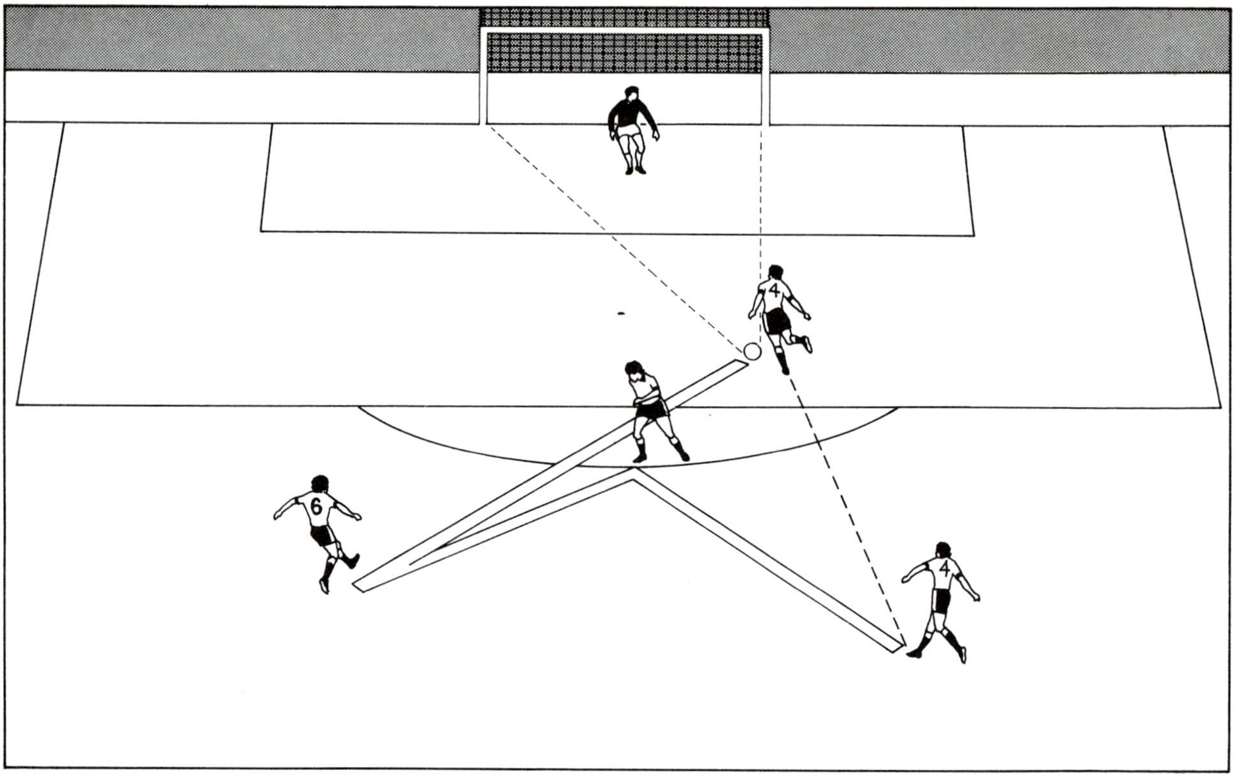
6
4
4

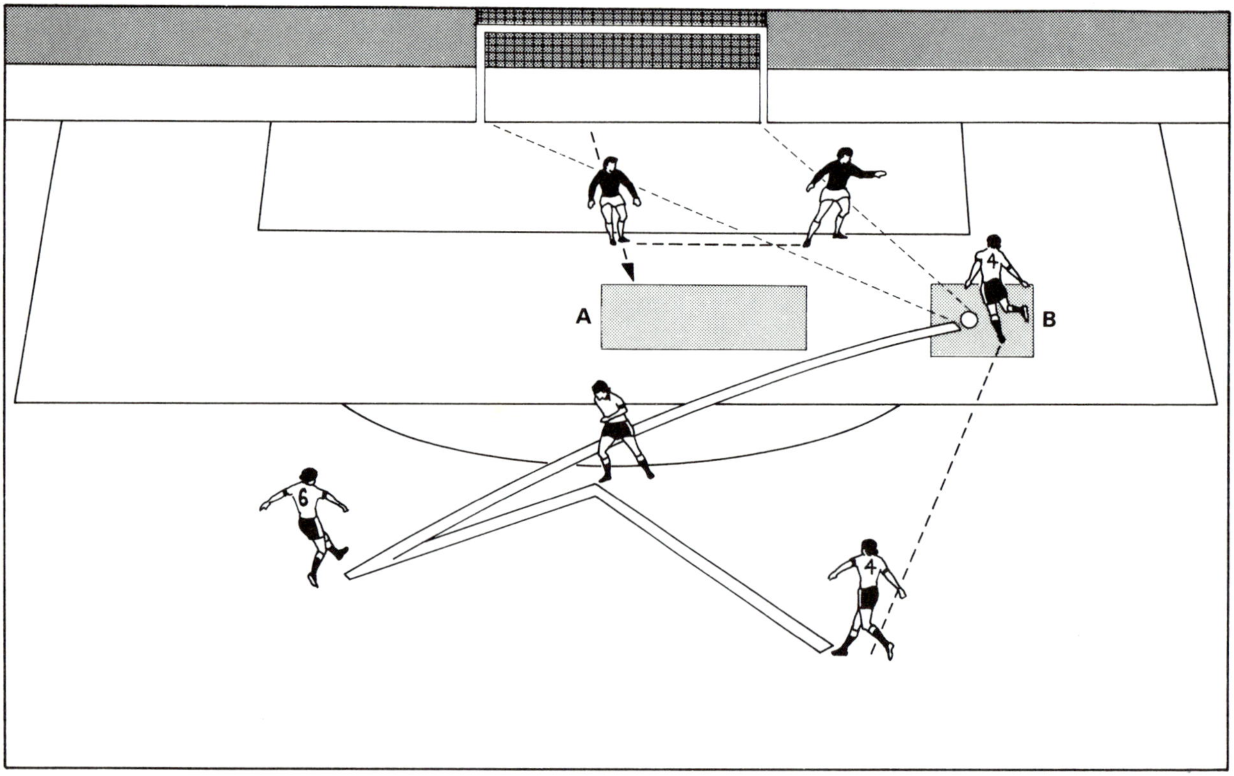
A
B
6
4
4

NO GO
AREA

What makes Shilton different to a lot of other goalkeepers? "I'm a great believer in people reading situations," he says. "I hate to see goalkeepers on their line, watching situations develop and then having to suddenly react to something."

The diagrams on the lefthand page provide a good example of Shilton's attitude to the game in this respect. They show an England training session, which manager Ron Greenwood organised with the aim of giving three of his players running-off-the-ball and shooting practice. The object of the exercise was for player No. 4 to pass to No. 6 and then run forward to receive the final pass inside the penalty area and have a shot.

Shilton, referring to the top diagram on the left, points out that he wasn't "quite switched on" at the start of the session. He was positioned too close to his goal-line, thus allowing

player No. 4 to get too close to his goal, too.

"I was giving him the initiative, all the scope in the world to bring the ball under control and knock it past me. Suddenly, I woke up – I wasn't going to allow them to dictate to me, so I started to anticipate that final ball into the box (bottom diagram left) and it caused them all kinds of problems, especially for the man making the final pass. He was forced to play a much wider ball, into area B as opposed to area A, and even then I was in the right position, on or around my six-yard line, to stop the shot.

"It can be argued that I ruined the session for the other players, but then I can't apologise for doing my job as a goalkeeper."

Shilton has developed, indeed, a style in keeping with his strong, assertive personality. He is very much the boss man within his team's defence, with

his colleagues adjusting their approach to the game to suit *his*. This is particularly evident in the positioning of Nottingham Forest defenders when they're facing corners (diagram above). The only Forest defenders in Shilton's six-yard box are those covering his near and far post areas (circled) and he explains:

"The six-yard box, and particularly the shaded area, is a no-go area as far as they are concerned. It's my domain, and generally our defenders keep out of it, even if it means two or three opponents being totally unmarked there. It's my job to get to the ball in the six-yard box and I can't do it if there are a lot of other bodies in there. The other advantage of leaving opponents in the six-yard box to me is that our lads can concentrate on picking up men making late runs from deep positions."

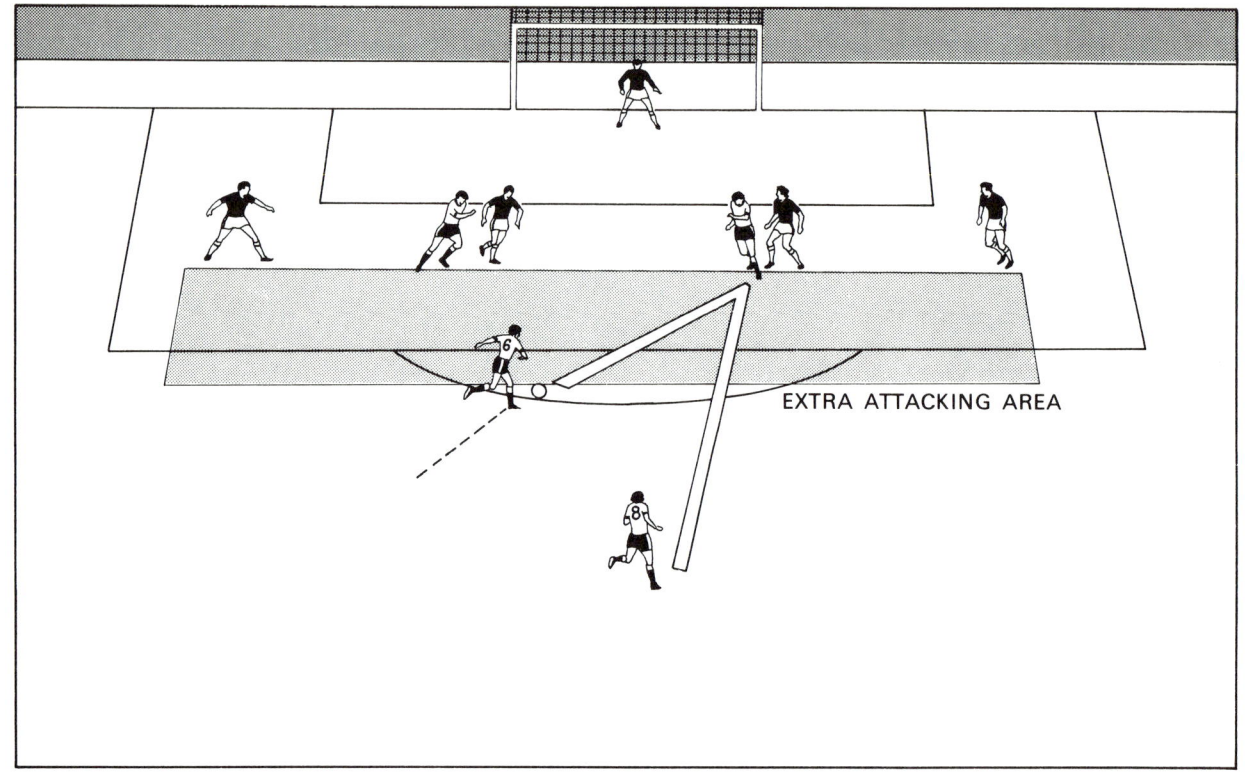

EXTRA ATTACKING AREA

Contrasting styles, or the Shilton method compared to that of many other goalkeepers. In the situation as illustrated here many goalkeepers tend to remain on their goal-line (diagram left) but Shilton would not – he'd move to the edge of his six-yard box (diagram right). "Because I come out and push the defenders immediately in front of me to the edge of the 18-yard box, opponents are forced to shoot from outside the penalty area, not inside."

Thus in the lefthand illustration, the goalkeeper and his defenders, through their anxiety to protect their goal, have unwittingly given their opponents the opportunity to get inside the 18-yard box. And in the righthand illustration, Shilton and his back four troops have denied their opponents that space. "We've adopted a more positive attitude to the

Generally, Shilton is proud of his overall image, although as he points out, it would count for precious little if he wasn't consistently living up to it through his performances. And one aspect of the technical side of his game which separates Shilton from a number of other goalkeepers is his ability to anticipate situations. "I'm a great believer in people reading situations," he says. "I hate to see goalkeepers on their line, watching situations develop, and then having to suddenly react to something."

There was a good example of what Shilton means during a recent England training session. Manager Ron Greenwood organised an exercise involving Shilton and three other players, designed to give the outfield men third-man running and shooting practice. The three players were lined up just outside Shilton's penalty box and the object of the exercise was for player 'A' to pass to player 'B', then run forward to receive the final pass – from player 'C' – inside the box and have a shot.

"I wasn't quite switched on," Shilton recalls. "The shots were coming in from between the penalty spot and the edge of the box and, with me being only two or three yards off my line, I was having to react to them. I thought: 'This is not right . . . you're allowing them to dictate to you.' So what I did was move further off my line, looking for the ball to be played into that space so that I was dictating to *them*."

Shilton's assertiveness is well illustrated by the amount of space between him and his back four men. They must sometimes feel as if they are operating in front of a human tank. Whereas other goalkeepers are inclined to remain on or near their

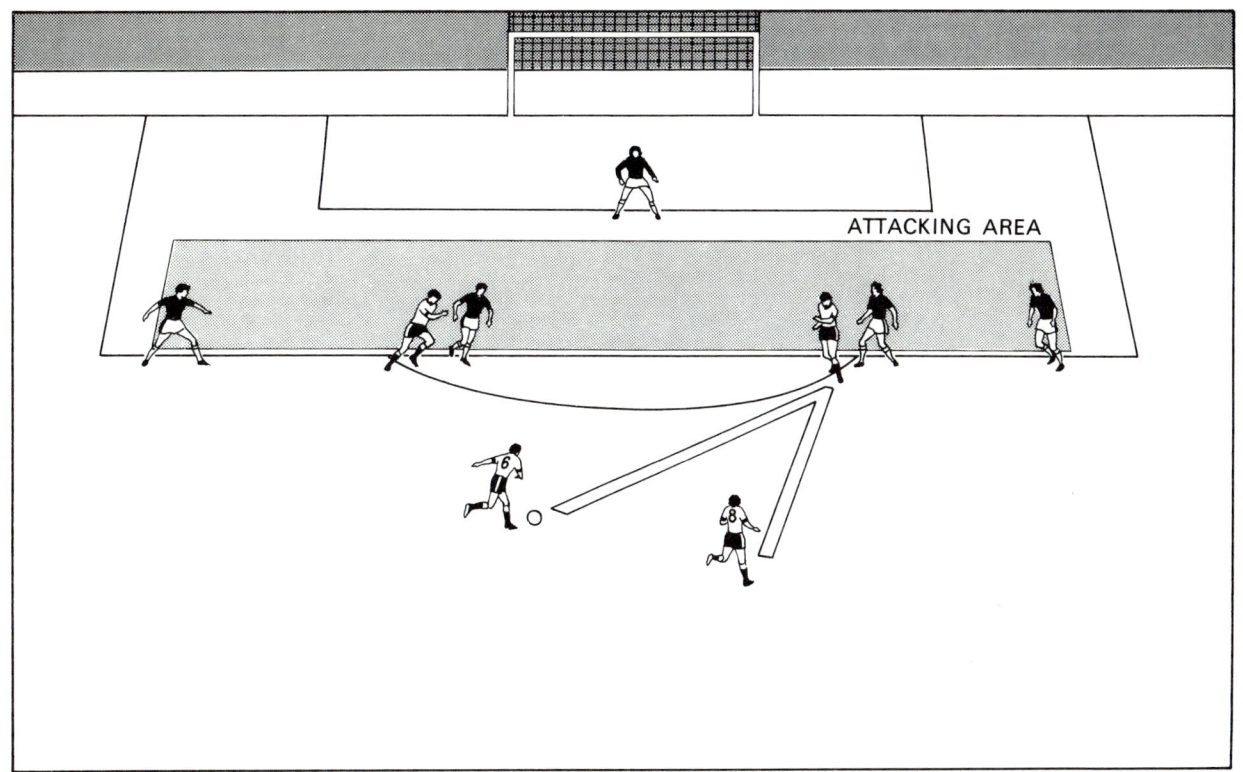

ATTACKING AREA

situation," he argues.

What problems has this created for the opposing No. 6 or No. 8? "He might attempt to thread the ball into the space between the Forest defenders and myself, but apart from the fact that I'd be looking out for that, it would be exceptionally difficult for the man for whom the pass is intended to get on the end of it without being offside. I don't think he could blast the ball past me from that distance – let's face it, it's much more difficult to score from 18 yards than from, say 12 yards, and he'd need to be a Pele to have much chance of chipping the ball over my head."

But says Shilton: "It's not easy to get defenders to move away from their goal. It means them going against their basic instincts. But having said that, I've yet to come across defenders who like conceding goals."

goal-line and allow their defenders to come back onto them, Shilton advances and commands his troops to go further forward and away from him.

It's also highlighted by the positioning of his defenders for corners. Forest have their full-backs covering the near and far post, like most other teams – but where they differ is that any opposing players standing in Shilton's six-yards box are not marked. One of the reasons for this is that Shilton is expected to catch any balls that come into that area, and his chances of doing so would inevitably be restricted if it was as crowded as Piccadilly Circus in the rush hour. Not only this, it ensures that Forest have plenty of men available to pick up opponents making late runs from deep positions.

"No matter how many opponents come into that six yards box, I just say to my defenders: 'Keep out

– it's my responsibility'.

"I think that all centre-halves like to be in contact with their goalkeepers because, in a sense, they feel vulnerable and insecure if they're not close to the goal," Shilton says. "Let's face it, it's their job to protect the goal, almost as much as it is the goalkeeper's job. They know that if anything goes wrong then they're second in line for the blame.

"I've always wanted my defence to build their tactical approach around me, not the other way around, although I must admit that there are certain cases in which the other way round has worked exceptionally well. Take the Leeds United team of the Sixties ... Gary Sprake wasn't the most commanding of goalkeepers and when the ball was flighted into his goalmouth, he'd be on his line with Jack Charlton in or around the six-yards box heading

Advantage to Shilton and his defenders as they move forward when under attack and with the ball being crossed from deep positions.

In the first illustration, the positioning of the goalkeeper and defenders means that their opponents have been able to get close enough to the goal to score with headers (1, 2), or a shot from a headed pass (3). Says Shilton disapprovingly: "The goalkeeper's attitude is: 'Well, I'm just going to stay on my goal-line and let the defenders deal with all the problems.' These are the sort of goalkeepers who, when they concede a goal in this situation, will look at their defenders as if to say: 'It's your job ... you should have cleared the ball.' They take the easy

it clear. Leeds didn't concede many goals, but for my money, it could have been even better if the goalkeeper had been taking charge. For me, goal-keeping is more about pushing everybody out and saying: 'Right, this is my area and I'm going to dominate it'."

But not all 'keepers are strong enough to cope with this extra responsibility. Shilton agrees that while most managers and coaches accept the advantages of creating that gap, or "no-man's land" as he calls it, between their 'keeper and defenders, "silly mistakes occur on the field because there's no real authority there.

"Managers and coaches can't stop these errors," he adds. "You can only stop them by having a good goalkeeper."

Another problem revolves round the responsibility of centre-halves to protect their goal. The men who fill the No. 5 spot tend to be strong-minded, obstinate characters who don't take too kindly to being told to go against their basic instincts. Shilton admits that he initially had his battles with Dennis Smith at Stoke, and it was the same with Larry Lloyd at Nottingham Forest.

Lloyd, formerly with Bristol Rovers, his home city club, Liverpool and Coventry, has much in common with Shilton. Though much more excitable than Shilton, he is just as determined and stubborn.

That stubborness led Lloyd into conflict with Brian Clough on more than one occasion. One day, towards the end of his spell at Forest, when he was called into Clough's office to explain a row he'd had with Peter Taylor during a close-season tour, Clough began by asking Lloyd if he liked him.

NO GO
AREA

way out and, to me, it's all wrong."

In the second illustration, showing the positioning of Shilton and his men in these instances, such scoring attempts (2, 3) are being made further from the goal and are thus much less dangerous. Shilton's insistence on having extra space in which to work, a "no go" area for his defenders, does not make it easy for opponents to hit crosses behind his men (1, 4) because he has also advanced, to the edge of his six-yard box. "The only other option for the man on the ball is to try and beat me with a chip (5) over my head. But I would be anticipating that and would need to take only a few steps back to get to the ball."

"What do you mean?" Lloyd replied. "As a manager or a person?"

"Never mind about that," Clough persisted. "Do you like me?"

Lloyd thought about it for a while and then said: "Well, as a manager I respect you more than any other man I've ever come across in the game, but as a person I wouldn't stand at the bar of my local with you."

When Lloyd joined Forest, he recalls that he "latched onto Clough like a parasite." His spell at Coventry had gone sour and he says that he needed a strict manager like Clough "to let me know who's the boss." He adds: "Some people are winners, others are losers and I knew Clough was one of the winners."

Perhaps that partly explains why Lloyd was prepared to be "managed" on the field, too, by that "human tank" called Shilton.

There were problems at first. "It was a battle of personalities," Shilton says. "With Larry, it was a matter of saying: 'Look, I appreciate the way you are, but I'm the goalkeeper and there's no way you're going to get the better of me'." More importantly, Shilton gained Lloyd's respect, not just for his ability, but his honesty, his willingness to accept the blame on those occasions when his goalkeeping philosophy and methods back-fired and the ball landed in his net. "Larry and the other lads knew that if I'd made a mistake I'd be the first person to hold his hand up in the dressing room afterwards and say: 'My mistake, sorry.' This means so much to me ... It's so important to me to be totally honest with the players around me."

Lloyd, who of course operated in front of Ray Clemence at Liverpool, says that Shilton prefers more space in front of him than Clemence. Occasionally, Lloyd felt that Shilton went to the extreme. "As the ball was being cleared out of our box, 'Shilts' would be shouting 'Out', 'Out', ... then 'Keep going,' 'Keep going'. I didn't want my lack of pace to be exposed, so I'd be thinking: 'No, I think you've gone far enough'.

"Generally," Lloyd says, "I tried to strike the happy medium between what he wanted and what I wanted and, fortunately, it worked well."

Says Shilton: "I know what I can do and what I want my defence to do, and I think they're quite happy to go along with that. I've never come across a defence which likes conceding goals."

So why is it that Shilton's approach to the game (or the approach he's tried to instil into his outfield defenders) has been so effective? Basically, one of the advantages of Forest's system is that their back four, through moving out to within six yards of the edge of the 18-yards box, force opponents to make goal scoring attempts from that distance. "There's much more chance of a team beating the goalkeeper from, say, six yards than 12," Shilton points out.

Many top teams have been frustrated by Forest's system, and none more so than Hamburg in the European Cup Final. Forest's defence instinctively began to move out when Hamburg's international right-back Manny Kaltz, taking a square pass from Felix Magath on the left, mis-hit a 25-yard shot to Jurgen Milewski. Their discipline meant that Milewski was fractionally offside when he himself tried to beat Shilton, and therefore Shilton's superb save and Willie Reimann's alertness in putting the rebound into the net counted for nothing.

Opponents inevitably attempt to exploit the space in front of Shilton by having men running into it for balls hit over the top of Forest's defence. But, apart from the problem of having to time their runs perfectly to avoid being caught offside, the men striving to get on the end of those passes must also contend with Shilton's ability to read the game and, of course, his powerful image.

Many people in the game consider that it's in these one-against-one situations, when a player is clean through with only Shilton to beat, that the goalkeeper really excels.

It was the same with Ray Clemence when Clemence was at Liverpool. They, too, are renowned for the way that they push up on opponents, leaving the goalkeeper to cover the area behind his defence like a sweeper, although Shilton feels that they occasionally exaggerate this style of play, thus giving

---

The confrontation between a goalkeeper and opposing attacker is often a battle of wits ... and that's particularly true in a "one-against-one" situation. It's at times like these, when a man is bearing down on Shilton's goal with the ball, with only him to beat, that Shilton's imposing physique, stature in the game and confidence can demoralise even the most accomplished of opponents.

When his team are defending, Shilton is a great believer in his back four men advancing so as to keep opponents as far away from his goal as possible. But, as seen in the top illustration on the right, they have moved out too far ("They should have been 10–15 yards deeper inside their own half.") and an opponent has managed to get to a ball in the space behind them without being offside.

On the face of it, the goalkeeper has virtually no chance of keeping the ball out of his net. But Shilton, an outstanding reader of the game with an ice-cool temperament, is renowned for the number of times he comes out on top in these situations. "There's no way the goalkeeper could get to that through ball before the attacker," Shilton points out, "so it's a question of letting the attacker come at him and trying to out-think him. The longer the attacker holds onto the ball, the more chance the 'keeper has."

In the top illustration the goalkeeper, on the edge of the penalty area when the ball was played through, retreats to the edge of his six-yard box as the attacker moves into an area in which he'll be considering chipping the ball over the goalkeeper's head. Once that possibility has been discounted, the goalkeeper can advance with more confidence, "But not too quickly," Shilton stresses, "otherwise the attacker is liable to slip the ball past him with a low shot close to his feet."

The 'keeper's ultimate aim, Shilton says, is to create a situation whereby the only way the attacker can beat him is to dribble the ball around him. Then as shown in the bottom illustration: "The goalkeeper doesn't commit himself until it is absolutely necessary for him to do so. Suddenly, all the odds are stacked in his favour and the attacker just cracks."

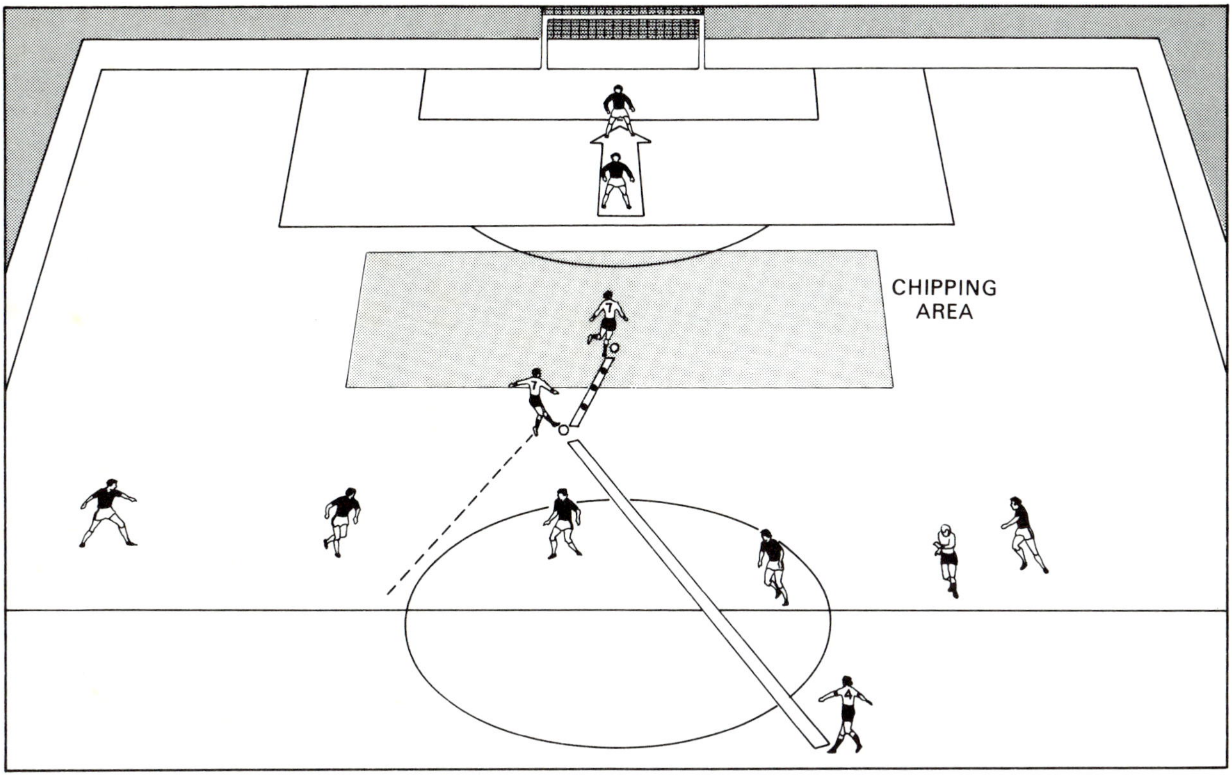
CHIPPING
AREA

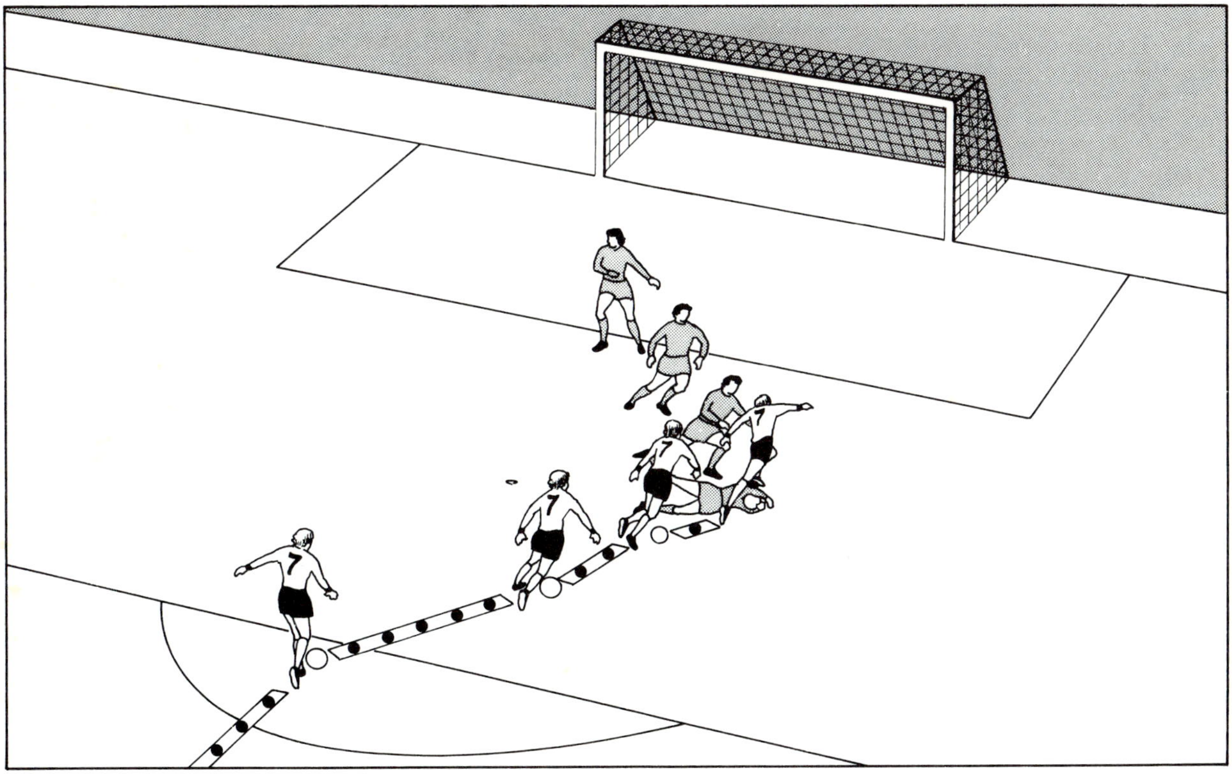

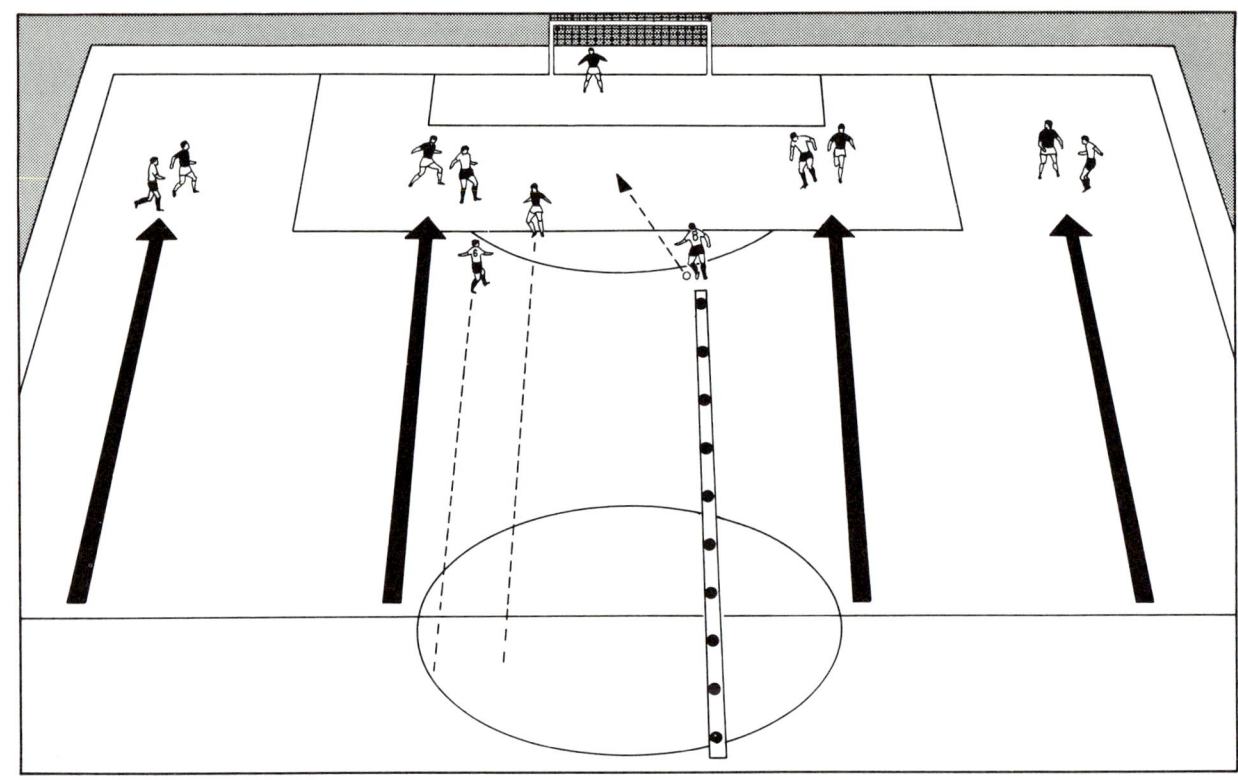

"Some of my best matches," Shilton says, "have been those in which I haven't had a shot or header to save." An exaggeration, perhaps, but Shilton finds it irksome that, like other goalkeepers, he's often judged on only his physical contribution to a match.

The above illustrations provide an example of how Shilton, through his knowledge of the game and willingness to take on the responsibility of organising his defence, can stop potentially dangerous situations developing.

In the lefthand diagram, the back four men have allowed their opponents to stretch them across the field, thus leaving a lot of space in the middle. Says Shilton: "Their attitude is: 'Well, I've got my man and am not really worried about anyone else.' But as a goalkeeper, you can see the overall picture

the 'keeper too much ground to make up. There was an example in the second Arsenal-Liverpool FA Cup semi-final replay in 1979/80, when Arsenal's goal in a 1–1 draw was scored by Alan Sunderland with a lob over Clemence as the 'keeper attempted to smother the ball at his feet.

"Liverpool's defence left Ray with an impossible task because there was no way he was going to beat Sunderland to the ball," Shilton says. "Ray is conditioned to racing out of his goal to get to a ball before an opponent, and in that particular instance I think it worked against him. On reflection, I'm sure he would agree that he'd have been better off to hold his ground, allow Sunderland to gain full control of the ball and then try and psych him into a bad shot."

More recently, there was another example, in the

1981 European Cup final against Real Madrid in Paris, of how Clemence commits himself in one-against-one situations, although on that occasion his opponent hit the ball narrowly over the bar. "He really should have scored," Shilton says. "It's a question of striking the right balance, doing what the particular situation demands."

Shilton himself is a master when it comes to forcing opponents to make the first move. "He is absolutely outstanding in one-against-one situations," enthuses former Leicester assistant manager, Bert Johnson. "Some goalkeepers will come out and virtually give the goal away – you know they're on the floor long before the fellow on the ball has got to them; they're just going through the motions, grovelling there in front of the man and making his mind up for him. Watch Peter Shilton in these

and there's no point in defenders going tight on opponents in certain areas if it means other attackers are able to get into good positions."

In the righthand diagram, is demonstrated the way a goalkeeper like Shilton will pull his back four men closer together, even at the expense of one of the full backs leaving his opponent unmarked. "By tightening up the middle of the defence, you are not only cutting out the most dangerous part of an attack, but slowing the attack down to give other members of your team the chance to get back into covering positions."

Shilton takes enormous pride in this aspect of his game. "The people in front of you aren't dummies," he stresses, "but it's astonishing how much you can help a defence by shouting the right things, at the right times and in the right tone of voice."

situations – it's an education." Gordon Banks, no slouch in that department either (his ex-manager Matt Gillies claims that he deliberately licked his fingers to put his opponent off) rates Shilton the hardest 'keeper to beat in Britain. "It's incredible the way he can out-think players, make them do exactly what he wants them to do," Banks says.

Shilton, who not surprisingly worked on this aspect of his game as a youngster, has acquired a deep insight into the doubts that can go through an opponent's mind in these situations.

"The more time he holds onto the ball, the more chance you've got," Shilton explains, making it all sound ridiculously simple. "I think it's important for a goalkeeper to look confident because players do look up when they're running at you with the ball, and you've got to pressurise them in every way you can. That's very important, that word 'pressurise'. Initially, you've got to advance at the right speed, get up to him without him being given the chance to chip the ball over your head or hit it past you. All the time he's been looking up and thinking: 'Chip him . . . No,' 'Whack it past him . . . No,' and all of a sudden he's right on top of you and the only option he's got left is to try and take the ball around you."

What would be going through his opponent's mind at that stage? "Well, he's probably thinking about the presence and the reputation of the man he's facing," Shilton says. "Yes, an important word 'pressurise'."

5

THE
SAVING GRACE

Another great Shilton save, demonstrating the importance of "committing yourself to every shot."

Ipswich's manager Bobby Robson stood in the dressing room corridor at Portman Road digging his hands deeply into his pockets and muttering darkly about his team's failure to beat Nottingham Forest.

It was the opening match of the 1979/80 season and Forest, despite having played poorly and spent most of the 90 minutes entrenched in their own half, ended up winning 1–0 by virtue of Peter Shilton's brilliance. In a rare Forest attack Tony Woodcock had capitalised on a mistake by Ipswich 'keeper Laurie Sivell to get the decisive goal. At the other end Shilton produced three "world-class" saves – two at point blank range, from shots by Paul Mariner and finally from an exquisitely-struck curling shot by Clive Woods. The look on the faces of Mariner and Woods told its own story as did Bobby Robson's frown as he discussed the match with newspaper reporters.

"I said to my players before the game that when you get in front of Peter Shilton's goal don't think he is unbeatable, but he was just that." Robson said, shaking his head. He was asked whether he felt Shilton would have saved Forest's goal. "Probably," Robson replied, eyeing the questioner coldly, "but then Laurie Sivell isn't a Peter Shilton is he? There's only one Peter Shilton."

Robson's despair that day has been shared by many other managers because, although Shilton's ultimate aim is to organise and motivate his defence to the point of them stopping the ball reaching him, there are obviously matches when he is called upon to make as many outstanding saves as any 'keeper. He succeeds more often than most. Shilton's ability to keep his teams in a game, virtually single-handed, has become almost legendary. There are few more common sights in English football than the glazed expression of disbelief on the faces of forwards after discovering that their best shots and headers haven't been good enough to get past him.

"It's never been enough for me to be just a solid, reliable goalkeeper," Shilton says. "Being solid and reliable is a big asset, but you want to be able to perform a few miracles from time to time, too.

"I hate it when people say: 'Oh, the goalkeeper had no chance with that goal.' Now obviously it's right in some cases, but sometimes I see 'keepers let in so-called wonder goals which I've known damned well they could have stopped if they'd been good enough. It's all about attitude as well as ability isn't it? I see goalkeepers facing shots in training and they let certain balls go or don't make too much of an effort to get to them. Some do it in matches . . .

now that's wrong . . . you should go for everything; even with shots which are going a yard or two wide, you should still make the effort to dive and cover the goal. I know that in training it sometimes looks a bit flash but it's not flash, it's making sure you are committing yourself to every shot."

To Shilton, the importance of that attitude was borne out by some of his saves in the European Cup Final against Hamburg. For example, there was the 25–30 yard shot from Bernd Nogly, which seemed to swerve slightly to Shilton's right around the penalty spot, and then bent left towards the top left hand corner of Shilton's goal. Shilton, having had to change direction, went for the ball with his left hand, but then, realising that he wasn't going to get it that way, brought his other arm across, while in mid-air, to give himself extra momentum and pushed it away with his right, for a corner.

From the corner on the right, Horst Hrubesch flicked the ball on with his head, into the goalmouth, and Milewski was poised to apply the finishing touch with a header from the edge of the six-yards box when Shilton dived forward to punch the ball away. "Something just told me I had to go for that flick-on," Shilton says. "I just came out and dived, without realising at the time that Milewski was there. I was very proud of the save, firstly because I anticipated Hrubesch's header and secondly because of the speed with which I reacted to the situation. The other thing is that I could easily have had my head knocked off, but of course you don't think of such things at the time."

Milewski went even closer to beating Shilton when Kevin Keegan chested the ball down to him in the box, and he hit what Shilton describes as a "perfect" first-time shot on the half volley, which seemed certain to go just inside the 'keeper's left-hand post. "He managed to keep the ball low and, being a bit unsighted, I saw it too late for my liking," says Shilton. For a split second he felt that the ball was going to go past him. "I've watched it quite a few times on my video and still can't quite believe that I managed to keep the ball out."

It's at moments like those that Shilton feels "high", as if he's on drugs. "About ten times a season," he says, "I'll make a save which will stem, not just from my training, but from something I've been born with. I surprise myself and when that happens I get a feeling of elation, as opposed to satisfaction."

All managers and coaches appreciate the psychological advantages of having goalkeepers capable of performing "miracles". As Shilton points out

NOGLY

SHILTON

Two of the most memorable Shilton saves occurred in the 1980 Nottingham Forest–Hamburg European Cup Final. As a result, Forest, out-classed for much of the match, ended up winning 1–0.

In the left-hand illustration is depicted Nogly's ferocious, swerving shot from outside the penalty area. "Goalkeepers are normally *expected* to save shots from that distance," Shilton says, "but this was an out-of-this-world shot!" An out-of-this-world save, too.

Nogly hit the ball exceptionally hard and Shilton was a little unsighted by the players in front of him. "The other problem was that the shot started going to my right and

matches can be won and lost on just one outstanding save because, apart from keeping the scoreline unchanged, it can so often have the effect of lifting one team and demoralising the other. "As a goalkeeper one of the things you are aiming at is to frustrate the opposition, make them respect you – even fear you – to the extent that if you do make one or two out-of-the-ordinary saves in a match, they will suddenly *go*. I've established a fair reputation of being able to do this sort of thing. I'm not superhuman, but when I'm really on song I do sense opponents thinking: 'How the hell are we going to beat him?'"

What many people in the game don't appreciate, Shilton argues, is that goal-stopping can be just as exciting to spectators as goal-scoring. "I feel very strongly about this. It's often said that the main way

to make the game more attractive to the general public is to give them more goals, but for me, a 0–0 match, in which both goalkeepers are making great saves, can be as enjoyable to watch as any high-scoring game."

People interested in football usually remember great goals rather than saves, although the obvious exception concerns the performance of Gordon Banks in England's 1970 World Cup quarter-final against Brazil in Mexico and, more specifically, his extraordinary save from Pele.

Brazil, the 1970 World Cup winners, did much to make the competition compulsive viewing with their flamboyant attacking football. But when discussing that year's tournament today, people will often recall not so much the flair of Pele, Gerson, Jairzinho, Rivelino and Tostao – and the superb

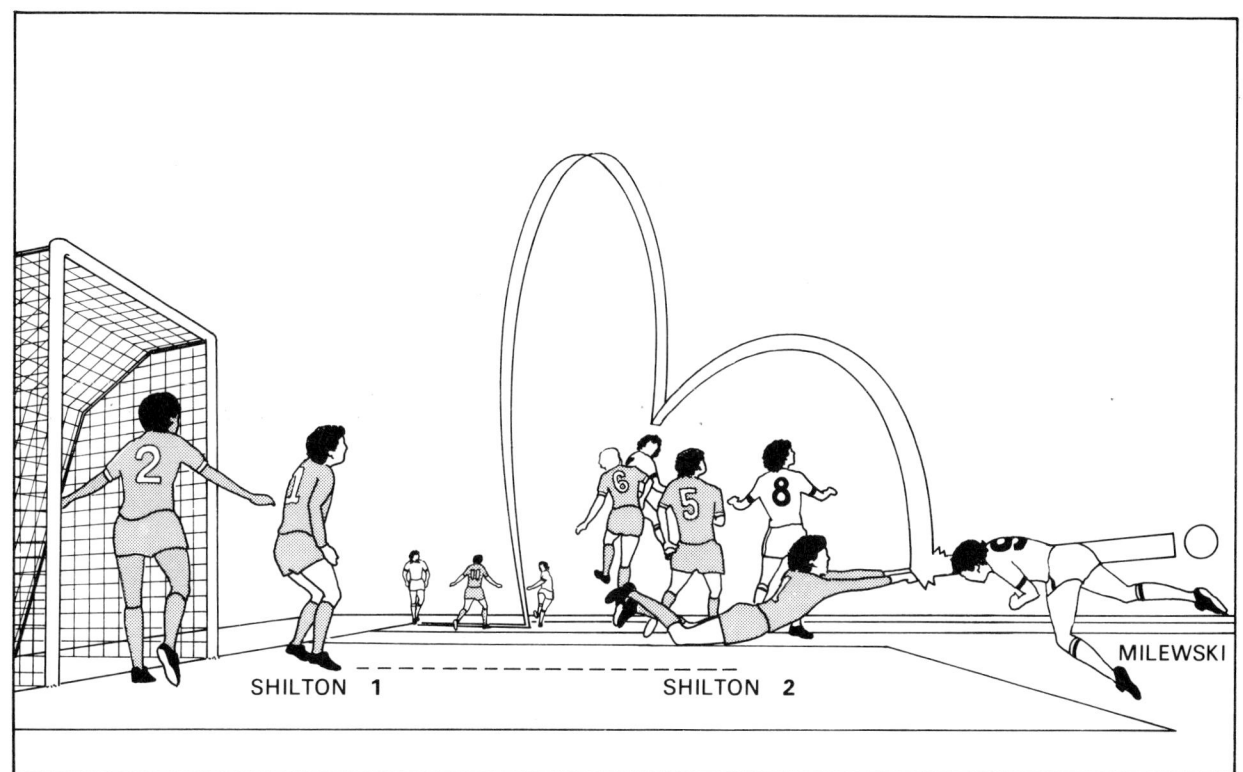

SHILTON **1** SHILTON **2** MILEWSKI

then went to my left," he re-calls. "I couldn't get into position quickly enough to save it with my left hand, so I had to bring my other arm across, while in mid-air, to give myself extra momentum and push the

ball away with my right."

From the resulting corner (illustration right), Hrubesch headed the ball on to the edge of the six-yard box where Milewski, having originally been on Shilton's goal-line, was

poised to apply the finishing touch. But Shilton ("Something just told me I had to go for that flick-on.") has moved out to punch the ball away a split second before Milewski could make contact.

goals in the quarter-final against West Germany (4–3) and final against Italy (4–1) – but the way such men were frustrated by Banks. Countless words have been written about that save from Pele in the 10th minute, and it was particularly well illustrated in a book: "World Cup 1970" edited by Hugh McIlvanney and Arthur Hopcraft:

"Carlos Alberto gave the ball along the right to Jairzinho and the winger accelerated dramatically beyond Cooper to the bye-line. From there his centre was pitched towards the far post, some seven or eight yards out. Pele, reading the situation flawlessly and moving as perhaps only he could, had come in on the far side of Mullery and now he rose, in an elastic leap, arching his back and neck to get behind and above the ball. The header was smashed downward, with vicious certainty aimed just inside

the upright Banks had been obliged to neglect as he went to the near post in an effort to cover Jairzinho's cross. Pele, Mullery reported later, shouted 'goal' as the ball flew off his head. So did nearly everyone else in the stadium. But Banks, hurling himself back across his goal, at a speed that will never cease to awe those who were there or the millions who watched on TV, was already twisting into range as the ball met the ground two or three feet from his line. When it rose again venomously, he managed to flick his right hand at it and divert it miraculously over his cross-bar."

Shilton has always had a grudging admiration for Banks's feat that day, grudging because it firmly established him as the No. 1 goalkeeper in the world, a status which Shilton feels he would have attained had one of his great saves been on a similar football

canvas. When discussing the impact of Banks's proudest moment, he says: "It came at the right time, the right place and against the right player." Not for one moment though, does Shilton attempt to detract from the technical aspect of the save. "I can't say it's the greatest save I've ever seen," he says, "because I've seen so many of them and it's very very difficult to try and separate them. But it was certainly one of the best, for a number of reasons."

Shilton explains: "The first thing is that it's always difficult for a goalkeeper to deal with crosses from on or near the goal-line. Usually the man on the ball is really stretching to get it across, maybe a bit off balance, and it can go anywhere." Banks was half expecting the ball to go to the near post. "Initially that's the area you've got to think about covering in these situations," Shilton says. And apart from the fact that Jairzinho's cross to the far post was perfectly struck, another problem for Banks was that Pele was shielded by Mullery. But while that robbed Banks of a split second of reaction time, Shilton suggests that it was made up by the ball bouncing in front of him.

The Shilton save which immediately springs to Banks's mind, was the one against Liverpool's Kenny Dalglish in the last few minutes of an England-Scotland match at Wembley in May 1973, when Shilton denied Dalglish in the same unorthodox way as he did Hamburg's Nogly. "The ball was travelling at a hell of a speed into the top left hand corner and, with players in front of him, his view of the ball was limited," Banks recalls. "How he got there I just don't know."

Former Leicester assistant manager Bert Johnson and Stoke manager Tony Waddington are both left scratching their heads when asked to name Shilton's best saves. "He's made so many of them," Johnson says, "that after a while you become blasé and only remember his mistakes."

"If any other 'keeper had been in our team in the European Cup Final," says Forest's assistant manager Peter Taylor, "we'd have been thanking and praising him for months afterwards. But with Peter, well, quite honestly, we take it for granted. I said beforehand that one goal would be enough and, despite the pressure Hamburg put on us, there wasn't one period when I felt Peter wasn't capable of dealing with everything they threw at him."

There is one Shilton save, however, that stands out in Brian Clough's mind. It was from a shot by Trevor Francis – then with Birmingham City – when Forest won 2–0 at Birmingham in 1977/78. "It inspired *me*, so God knows what it did for the other players," Clough says.

Francis had his back to Shilton's goal, with a defender breathing down his neck, when the ball was played up to him on the left of Forest's penalty area, just outside the six-yards box, when he suddenly turned inside his marker and hit a ferocious rising shot towards the top right-hand corner of the net. But Shilton, having read the situation and come out to narrow the angle, not only blocked the shot with an outstretched left hand, but got enough power and leverage behind it to put the ball out of play for a corner. "It was a two-in-one save really," Shilton says, "because not only did I stop the shot but I also ruled out the possibility of anyone else sticking the ball in at the far post."

"It was one of my best saves ever." He adds: "Actually Trevor (who later joined Shilton at Forest) told me it was *the* greatest he'd seen."

There was another Shilton "miracle" towards the end of that season, which helped Forest draw 0–0 at Coventry City (Shilton's 22nd clean sheet in 33 matches) and get the point they needed to clinch the Championship. Ian Wallace dummied past a Forest defender on the right of the area and Shilton, who had been drawn to the near post, suddenly had to change direction as the ball was crossed into the middle for Mick Ferguson. Coventry's centre-forward was unmarked on the edge of the six-yards box and able to set himself up for a perfect header to the right . . . but Shilton readjusted yet again to push it over the bar.

One of Shilton's most crucial saves came in the first half of Forest's 3–2 win over Southampton in the 1979 League Cup Final. Southampton forward Phil Boyer and a Forest defender collided when challenging for a low cross and Shilton had to dive

---

A similar save to the one Shilton produced against Hamburg's Nogly, this time against Ken Dalglish in England's 1–0 win over Scotland at Wembley in May 1973. Gordon Banks rates it the greatest Shilton save he has seen. Here again, Shilton went for the shot (to his left) with his left hand but pushed it away with his right. "The ball didn't swerve as Nogly's shot did," Shilton says, "but Dalglish was closer to the goal when he hit it and, again, I was a little bit unsighted."

Banks recalls that Dalglish's shot was "travelling at a hell of a speed," and admits that he wouldn't have expected any goalkeeper, least of all himself, to get to it.

Shilton readily acknowledges the point: "About 10 times a season, I'll make a save which will stem not just from my training but from something I've been born with. I surprise myself and when that happens I get a feeling of elation as opposed to satisfaction."

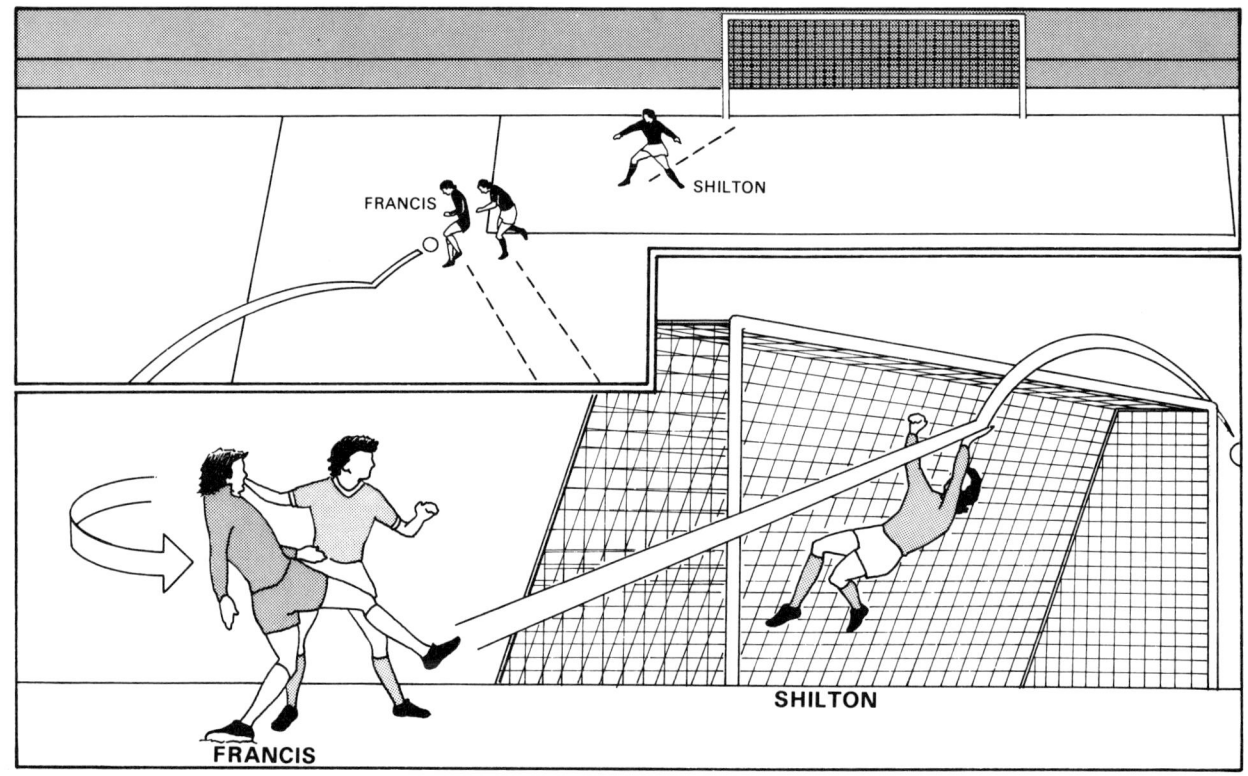

FRANCIS

SHILTON

SHILTON

FRANCIS

Left, Brian Clough's favourite Shilton save – from Trevor Francis in Nottingham Forest's 2–0 win at Birmingham City in December 1977.

"When you see a player in that situation," Shilton says, "you tend to expect him to lay the ball off rather than turn and get in a shot as Francis did. One of the things about that save which pleased me is that I didn't discount the possibility of him shooting, and moved off my line to narrow the angle as the ball was played to him. Then, I not only got my hand to the shot, but had enough strength in my arm and wrist to put the ball out of play – if it had still been in play, the

head-first at Mick Holmes's feet on the six-yards line ("with the boots flying around me") to prevent him turning the loose ball into the net. "I think Brian Clough went on record as saying that the save won us the League Cup," Shilton says. "Southampton had gone ahead about five minutes earlier and if that one had gone in I think we'd have been dead."

Among the one-against-one saves to have given Shilton the most satisfaction were those against Grasshopper Zurich's Claudio Sulser in the first leg of Forest's European Cup quarter-final in Nottingham in 1978/79 (4–1; 5–2 on aggregate) and, the following season, against Liverpool's David Johnson in the second leg League Cup semi-final at Anfield (1–1; 2–1 on aggregate). In the first, Sulser gained full possession of the ball from a long pass over the Forest defence and, as he advanced towards

Shilton, unleashed a volley to the left which the 'keeper – around 10 yards away, just outside his six-yards box – managed to turn away. In the second, when Johnson started his run for a through ball, the odds were 60–40 in favour of him getting to it first. "But I turned those odds into my favour," Shilton says. "I not only got to it a split second before him, but actually held it."

Not surprisingly for a man of his stature, there have been a fair number of Shilton penalty saves too. Among the most memorable was one he produced in an FA Cup fifth round replay at Liverpool in 1968/69. Tommy Smith was Liverpool's penalty taker in those days and noting that he had a tendency to place his shots to the right, Shilton spent 10 minutes in training the previous day facing spot kicks to that side. He got the chance to prove the

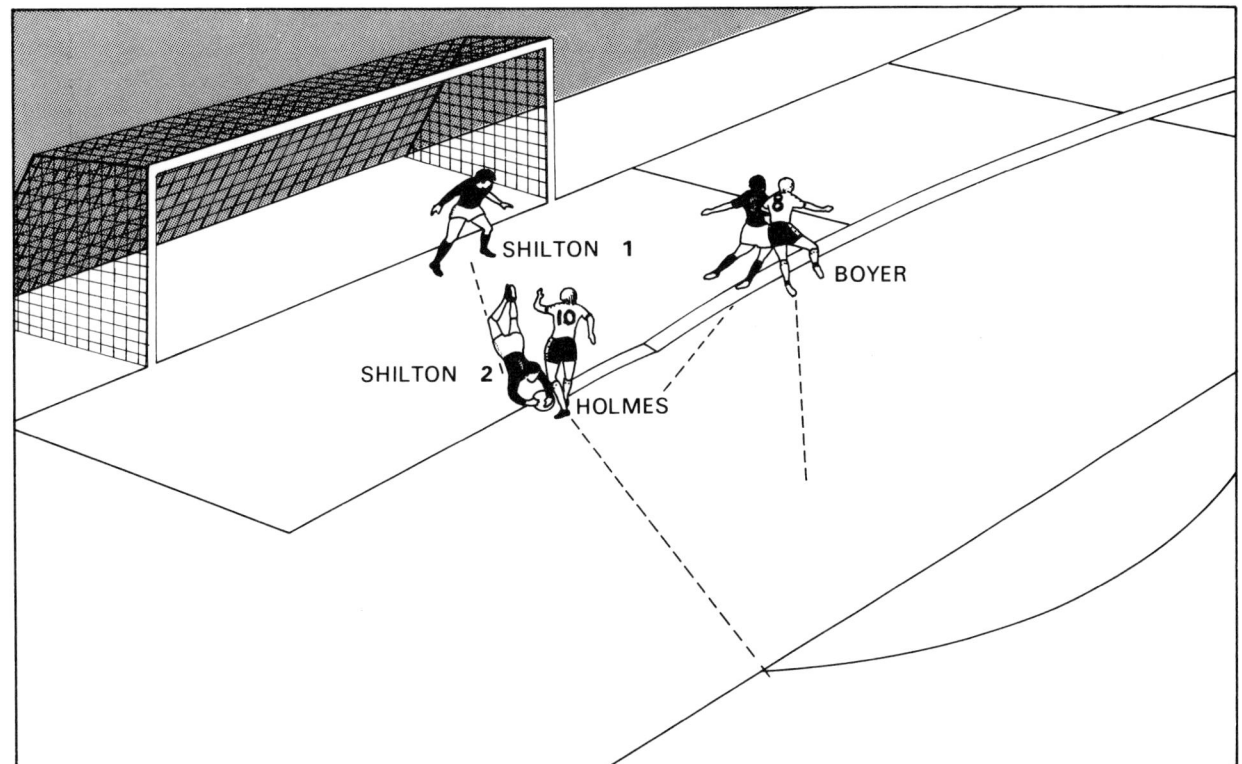

chances are that one of the Birmingham men following up would have stuck it in."

In the righthand illustration, Shilton's crucial save in the 1979 Forest–Southampton League Cup Final, when he bravely threw himself forward, head-first, to prevent Nick Holmes connecting with a low cross on the edge of the six-yard box.

"I had to react very quickly," Shilton points out. "The cross sort of went through Phil Boyer and the Forest defender marking him at the near post, and really Holmes had the slight edge on me in that situation." Forest, trailing 1-0 at the time, went on to win 3-2.

value of that work in the first half, five minutes after Andy Lochhead had given Leicester a surprise lead. Liverpool were awarded a penalty due to a hand-ball offence during a scramble in Leicester's goal-mouth, but Shilton timed his dive to perfection to knock the shot from Smith behind for a corner. Leicester held their lead and eventually got to the Final.

After joining Nottingham Forest, Shilton feels there was a period when he wasn't saving as many penalties as he could have done, a comment which further emphasises the pressure he puts on himself at times.

Shilton agrees that goalkeepers are "on a hiding to nothing" in these situations, and that they rely more on luck than ability but, at the same time, he insists that he sometimes contributed to his own

downfall through not being relaxed enough. It was Peter Taylor who initially pointed this out to him, suggesting that he was putting too much thought into anticipating where his opponent was going to put the ball and what type of shot he'd produce, as opposed to "just standing there with presence, like you normally do."

"He was right," Shilton says. "I was thinking too much about the technical side of it. That comes into it, obviously, but mainly it's a question of standing there as if to say: 'Come on, I'm Peter Shilton, try and beat me'."

While one would need a book with as many words as "War and Peace" to include all of Shilton's extraordinary performances over the years, no list of these would be complete without reference to Leicester's o–o draw on a quagmire of a pitch at

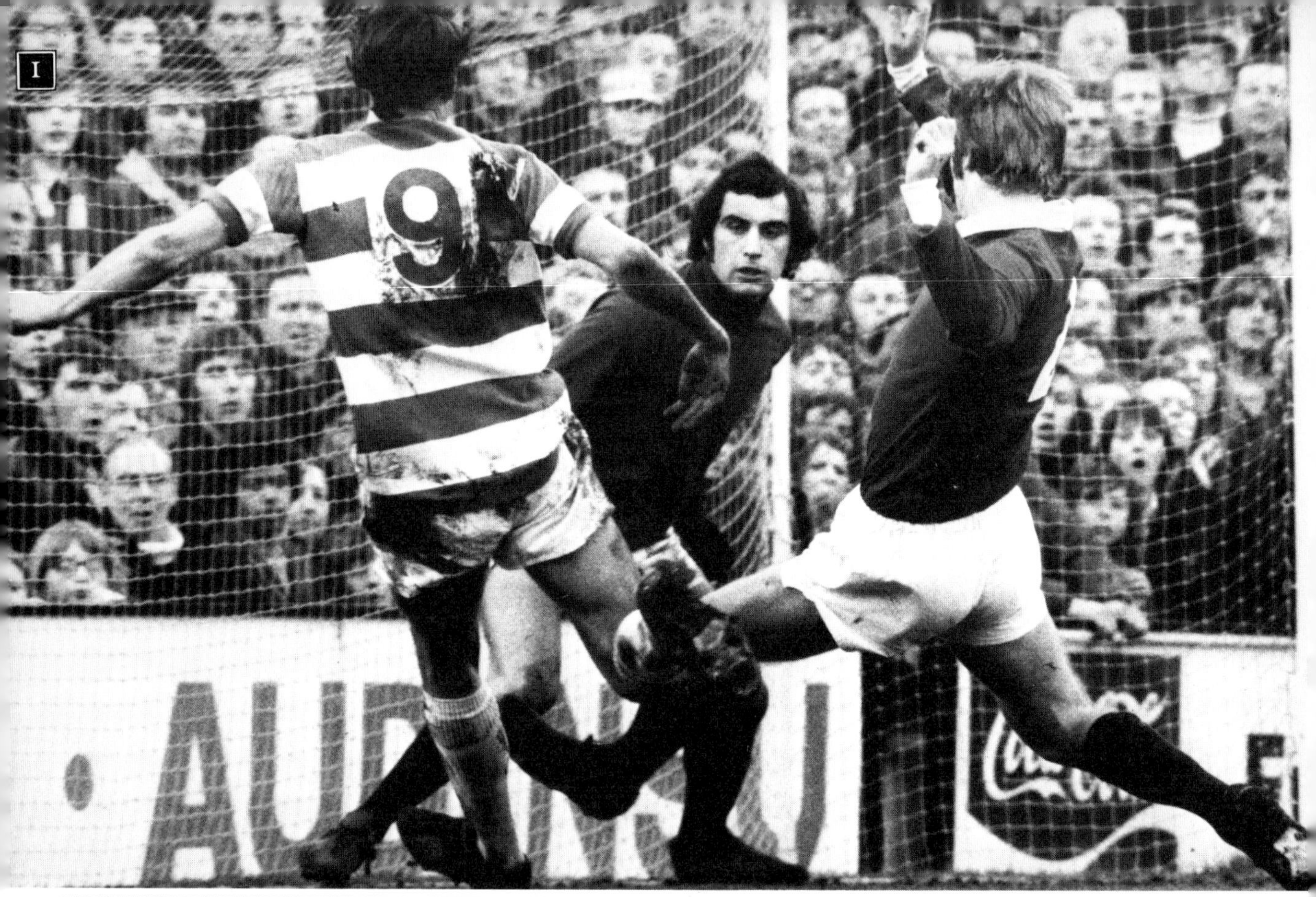

1

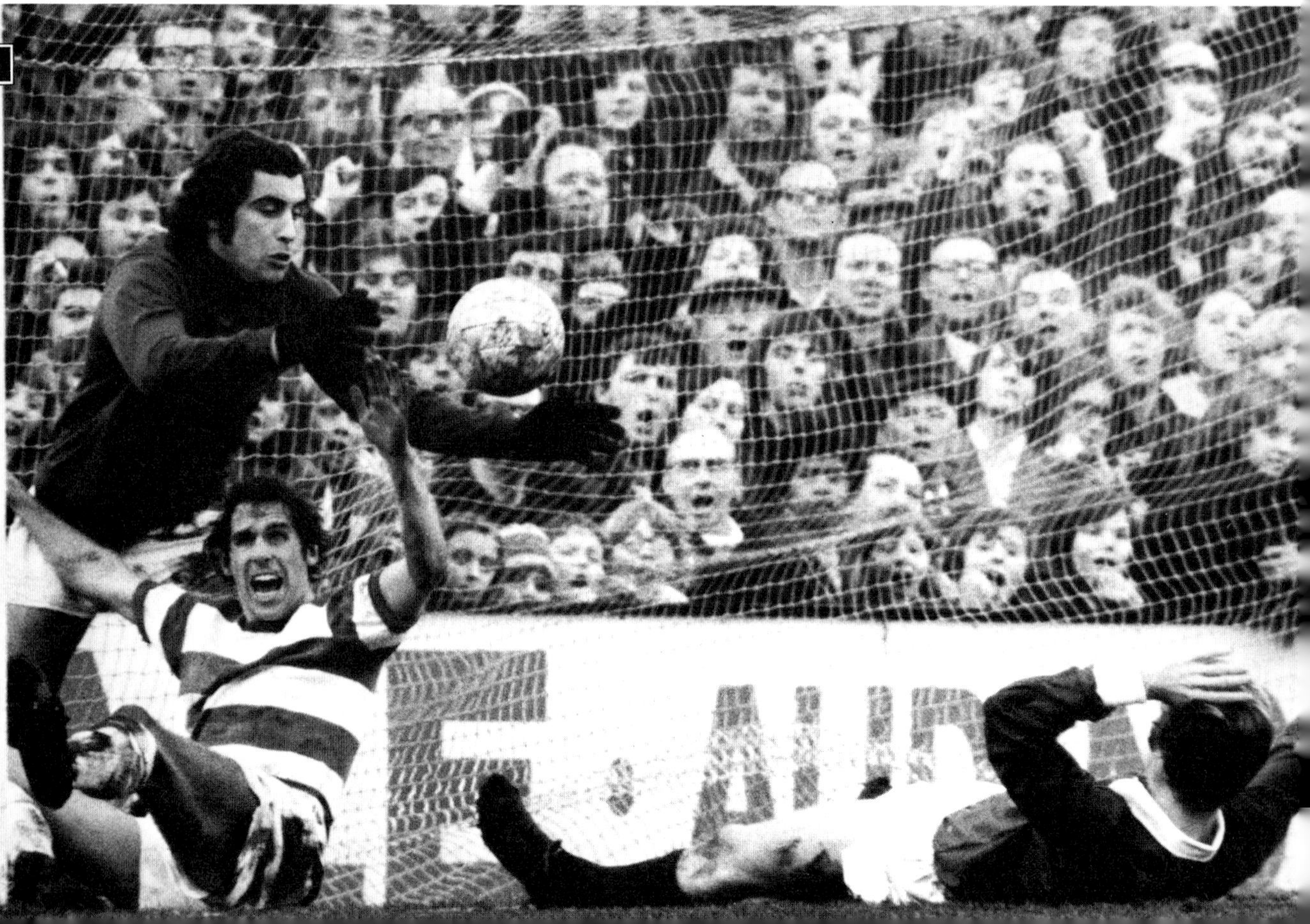

2

3

One of Shilton's greatest matches – Leicester's 0–0 draw at Queen's Park Rangers in 1974. He made so many outstanding saves that at the end even QPR's players applauded him off the field. One of the highlights is illustrated here:

1. Top left, opposite page, the ball is played across Shilton's goal and Leicester defender Steve Whitworth, at full stretch, gets a foot to it as Ranger's No. 9, Mick Leach, moves in for the kill.

2. Bottom left, Leach collides with Whitworth and, as the ball bobbles towards the net, collides with Shilton, too.

3. Above, the danger is averted, thanks to Shilton's physical power and determination.

Queen's Park Rangers in February 1974, and England's 1–0 win over Czechoslovakia on a hard, ice-bound Wembley surface in November 1978.

It's difficult to believe that Shilton has ever had more physical work to do during a match than that day at Queen's Park Rangers. The match was dominated by Shilton's almost unreal goalkeeping skills and as Brian Glanville observed in his report on the match for The Sunday Times: "At least seven of Shilton's saves were beyond the call of duty."

Rangers' striker Don Givens had an open goal after fastening onto a through pass and dribbling around Shilton, but the 'keeper took advantage of the time he'd created through pushing Givens wide, by pushing the ball away – from behind Givens – as he was about to apply the coup de grâce. Rangers' centre-half Terry Mancini too, was more than a little demoralised by a Shilton save from a close-range header, claiming afterwards that Shilton had "out-psyched" him.

"The man is actually 'selling dummies' to people trying to score," Mancini said. "It's unheard of. I had a great chance with a header and knew I just had to thump it square into the net. But he shaped to cover that side, so I glanced it for the other corner . . . and he was standing there laughing at me as he caught it. He's a magician."

An indication of how well Shilton performed that day is that at the final whistle, even the Rangers players applauded him off the field.

Czechoslovakia were as frustrated by Shilton's magic as Rangers had been. Despite the treacherous conditions, they produced some brilliant touch play that night and good chances too. It was Shilton's first international appearance under the management of Ron Greenwood and he more than justified the following day's "Shilton saves England" headlines, with four tremendous saves in the first half from shots by Zdenek Nehoda, Frantisek Stam-

bacher and Jan Kozak, and after England had taken a lucky second-half lead, a couple more from Marian Masny and Nehoda again. Shilton is particularly enthusiastic about his two saves just before half-time, when he "trapped" a Kozak shot on his goal-line, just inside his near post and then dived to the left to push away a powerful, swerving Nehoda shot from 20 yards. "Both difficult saves, if only because of the slippery conditions," Shilton says.

Neither of those QPR–Leicester and England–Czechoslovakia matches were shown on TV, much to Shilton's disgust. It's anybody's guess what he

● "I think this was one of three one-against-one saves I made in that QPR–Leicester match. It looks as if I've saved from Dave Thomas with my legs, but in fact I saved with my hands and the impetus of the shot knocked me backwards. Although the ball ran loose, I managed to get back on my feet quickly and fall on it before Thomas or another Rangers player could take advantage.

"I felt I did everything right on this occasion because as Thomas came towards me with the ball I didn't commit myself and got into a crouching position to spread myself. Eventually, with me covering most of the goal, he was forced to try and chip the ball over me.

"In this sort of situation, a lot of goalkeepers are inclined to sprawl a bit, and give the man on the ball the chance to hit it through them, but as you can see in the picture, I've kept myself extremely solid and compact. The body position is perfect.

"That save gave me a lot of satisfaction as Thomas was one of the best strikers of a ball in Britain at that time."

● "This was my best save in the QPR–Leicester match. People who watched the game still mention it to me today. Here again, it was a one-against-one situation, this time me against Don Givens. We both did the right things and in a way it was a pity that one of us had to lose out.

"As you can see, I'd held, and held and held long enough to allow Steve Whitworth to get behind me into a covering position but Givens then suddenly shaped to shoot, forcing me to dive, and took the ball around me instead. He was about to knock the ball into the net as I got off the floor and dived again, from behind him, to push the ball away with my right hand. It was real desperation stuff.

"I remember Givens just stood there dumbfounded – he couldn't believe it, As for me, well I'm the sort of person who never gives up – even in training, I go flat-out for *every* ball – and I like to think that save emphasised the advantages of this attitude."

would have given for such performances – and the one against Hamburg in the European Cup Final – to have been seen in the latter stages of a World Cup against players like Pele or Johan Cruyff or Diego Maradonna.

All of which brings us back to Gordon Banks.

It's fair to say that, like Shilton, Banks would also fill a key position in any British Goalkeepers' Lib society. He was never as outspoken or aggressive as Shilton in putting forward his members' cases for a better deal from people in the game and the general public, but what he did achieve through that duel

with Pele in the Mexico sun and, of course, his 1966 World Cup performances, was raise the image of his English League colleagues in the eyes of people abroad. The overall standard of British goalkeeping was regarded as the highest in the world before Banks came on the scene, but he reinforced it to the extent that only the most insular would have dreamt of quibbling with that view.

Banks's greatest attribute was his positional sense and anticipation which, in the words of Mark Wallington, enabled him "to make it look as though many shots had been fired straight at him." That,

● "My other one-against-one save, again from Don Givens. I have unusually long arms – a characteristic which stems from the stretching exercises I did as a youngster – and that helped me a lot on this occasion.

"When faced with a scoring attempt from that sort of distance, goalkeepers are inclined to be vulnerable to low shots close to their legs but I've made it difficult for Givens to squeeze the ball past me through being so crouched. If I couldn't have saved it with my left hand, I'd have kept it out with my leg.

"Here again, I've kept on my feet for as long as possible. Instead of panicking and committing myself, I've more or less said to Givens: 'Well come on . . . you try and beat me'."

● "This shot on the turn by Gerry Francis was a difficult one for me. As with all shots on the turn, it could have gone anywhere and the other problem was the muddy conditions.

"A lot of goals are scored as a result of 'keepers failing to hold such low, skidding balls, which probably explains why the Leicester players in the picture are looking so anxious. But I wasn't worried at all . . . although I'd had to stretch for the ball, I kept my eyes on it all the time – even when I'd got to it – and look at the position of my hands. I had one hand behind the ball and the other over the top of it, so as far as I was concerned, there was no way that it was going to break away from me.

"But what really made that save possible was that I wasn't on my goal-line – I'd come out to narrow the angle and had Francis hit the shot fractionally further away from me, it would have gone wide."

according to Shilton, sums up one of the big differences between British and Continental goalkeepers. British 'keepers, he insists, are generally stronger physically and have greater all round technical ability than many of those in other countries. "Continental 'keepers stay on their line more and rely more on their agility and quick reactions, the result being that they are inclined to make easy saves look more difficult than they really are."

Shilton concedes that there have been some outstanding 'keepers outside Britain – two who come readily to mind being West Germany's Sepp Maier ("An unusual type of 'keeper, a little bit unorthodox") and Italy's Dino Zoff. Neither though is Shilton's type of 'keeper.

Maier, Shilton claims, was too erratic while Zoff, whose game was developed around the ultra-defensive Italian style of play, isn't commanding enough for his liking. "He's forced back too much. You rarely see him standing on the edge of his box, reading situations and dominating things."

In recent years, Shilton has noted a growing tendency for foreign goalkeepers to incorporate some of the typically British characteristics into their play. Among these players is the 27-year-old Basque, Luis Arconada, who plays for the San Sebastian club Real Socieadad and Spain. Shilton feels that Arconada is more "complete" than other foreign 'keepers he has seen. He particularly caught Shilton's eye when England beat Spain 2–0 in a friendly match in Barcelona in 1980 and then 2–1 in the European Nations Cup Final in Italy in 1980. In the latter match, Shilton most enjoyed a string of Arconada saves in quick succession, when he kept "bouncing up and down like a rubber ball."

However, in both those England matches, there were certain aspects of Arconada's game which Shilton interpreted as "weaknesses". He says: "When it came to dealing with crosses, I noticed that Arconada started his run from quite close to his line, and in fact began to come out before the ball had actually been hit. This meant that he was assessing whether or not he was going to try and take the ball while he was moving towards it. I personally prefer to see a goalkeeper start his run for a cross a bit further out and thus give himself a greater margin for any error of judgement.

"Also, in situations when an opposing player was put clean through, and Arconada had to take on the role of a sweeper, I feel that he occasionally came too far off his line too quickly. There was a good example of this in the first match against England in the way

Tony Woodcock scored our first goal. Woodcock held all the aces, I agree, but I do feel Arconada would have made it more difficult for him had he held his ground a bit more."

One thing about Arconada which surprises Shilton is that "he seems to be fairly consistent". That, he claims, is a rare quality in Continental 'keepers and it's the department in which he feels their British counterparts have the biggest edge over them. "We're much more solid and reliable."

Shilton attaches enormous importance to consistency. "You see goalkeepers who'll go out in a big match and play the game of their lives, but then the following week they'll make a right hash of something, do something absolutely stupid. For me, there's no satisfaction in producing the odd brilliant performance if your overall standard of play isn't reasonably high."

Shilton is fascinating to listen to on the subject of his own high standard of consistency over more than 15 years at the top. "It's pride in your performance," he explains. "After my first two seasons at Nottingham Forest, my performances were such that people were beginning to look upon me as almost invincible . . . *invincible*. Then all of a sudden, the team started playing badly. I went off the boil for a short period and I lost the image a little bit. Now that hurt me so much that I still feel a little sick about it even today."

The period to which Shilton refers came midway through the 1979/80 season when Forest, second in the First Division at the time, dropped to seventh as a result of a disastrous run in which they got a draw against Arsenal but lost to Southampton, Brighton, Derby County, Arsenal and Crystal Palace. Much of the attention was focused upon Shilton because Forest conceded 14 goals in those six matches (compared with 13 in the previous 19 and 16 in the subsequent 22) and should, to some extent he felt, have been directed at other departments of the team.

"I felt I was being used to take all the pressure off other players who weren't playing well, and resented it," Shilton recalls. In fact he confronted Brian Clough about it at a team meeting and told him: "I think it's diabolical that you should be saying certain things about me and not doing something about other players who are letting you down."

But Shilton was equally hurt that for the first time in his career he'd allowed himself to drop about 20 per cent below his normal standard, or his groove as he calls it. Why did it happen? Shilton says that he suddenly started experiencing a reaction to the intense pressures of striving to live up to that standard over such a long period. "It all suddenly hit me," he says. "I rebelled against the game a little bit, but the important thing is that I snapped out of it. People say: 'Oh, it was a bad season for Shilton' but that's wrong. All it was was a bad *period* in the season, that's all."

"It's impossible to be 100 per cent right all the time, when you're playing an average of two matches a week, but you've got to be close to it. That's especially true for a goalkeeper because it's such a vulnerable position. For example, I've seen Trevor Francis have some great games but in others I've thought: 'If you had played like that, we'd have lost 3–0.' I was only 20 per cent below 100 per cent during that period, physically and mentally, and that, together with the fact the team weren't playing well meant that balls were going past me so quickly it wasn't true.

"We all have our bad or not-so-good matches, but the way I look upon it is that if you go above your basic standard over a period of, say 10 matches and save 30-odd goals, then concede five by dropping below it over the next 10, you're still 25 goals up.

"That's why I get so irritated occasionally, when people put so much emphasis on the mistakes I make, although I suppose it's a back-handed compliment in the sense that I have set such high standards. It's all relative, I know, and I can't speak for other goalkeepers, but over a season I'm looking to be at between 85 and 100 per cent."

One of the reasons why Shilton has achieved this is that he has learned to regulate his preparation for matches throughout the season, to avoid going stale. "It's like driving a car up 200 miles of motorway," he suggests. "It's not necessary to do those 200 miles at 70 miles an hour to get to one's destination in a reasonable amount of time. Besides, by not easing up on the throttle a little, the chances are the car's going to get over-heated and break down."

Shilton drove himself flat-out at the start of his career but insists that it was important for him to go to the limit (and sometimes beyond it) then to establish a sound foundation in terms of technical skills and physical strength. It helped to give him a yardstick by which he could strike the right balance in later years. That balance, he says, is essential in modern day professional football, especially for men with successful clubs such as Nottingham Forest.

"You can only take so much," Shilton says. "That's where I think a number of clubs and players make a mistake. They'll train hard just for the sake of it, without any real thought as to why they're doing it."

Shilton considers that when players push themselves too hard in training, there is the danger of them reaching a stage where they can get into bad habits. It was a point he felt obliged to make to Manchester City's Joe Corrigan, England's third-choice goalkeeper behind Shilton and Ray Clemence during the international squad's preparations for the 1980 European Nations Cup Final in Italy.

"Every afternoon Joe was going out for extra training in a sweatsuit, and I could see he wasn't enjoying it," Shilton recalls. "Now, you don't necessarily have to enjoy your training, but it had been a long hard season for him and the more he was doing, the more tired he was getting, tired of seeing all those balls coming at him. To me, it was doing him more harm than good.

"I put as much into the game as any player, but from time to time I'll ease off for two or three days, go the other way. I'll eat and drink what I like, perhaps get sloshed one night and then, when I've got all the tension out of my system, I'll be building myself up again. There's always the danger of going a bit overboard, but I know how I've got to feel to produce a good performance – the physical and mental groove I've got to get into – and when I'm in one of my winding-down periods, I know exactly how far I can afford to get away from it.

"All right, occasionally it might mean that instead of being 90 per cent right on a Saturday, I'm 80 per cent right. But, if you're going to produce a consistently high standard of performance throughout the season, that's the way it's got to be."

WITNESS
FOR THE DEFENCE

The disquieting moment: Shilton, and every other goalkeeper, dreads

So many outstanding saves have been made by Peter Shilton that after a while one tends to remember *only* his mistakes. Shilton argues that it's the same with all 'keepers: their good moments are often taken for granted; their bad moments blown up out of all proportion.

It's at such times, with Shilton on his soapbox, protesting about the way goalkeepers' mistakes are taken out of perspective, that he really does seem like the leader of a Goalkeepers' Lib movement, and an extremely militant one at that. He is so sensitive about this aspect of his job his feelings of persecution border on paranoia, exacerbated by the fact that on the rare occasions he makes an error he feels he is judged more harshly than anyone.

"It's a price one has to pay for setting such high standards," he shrugs. "If I let in three goals and none of them have been my fault, I still get people pointing a finger at me and saying: 'You shouldn't concede three goals'. If one or two of them have been my fault, they love that, they really go to town on that. You take Ray Clemence – no disrespect to Ray, but people didn't say much at all when England lost 4–1 to Wales (at Wrexham in 1980) whereas if I'd been in goal that day, I think I would have been absolutely slated."

Shilton's tone of resentment stems partly from the stick he took during the period in the 1979/80 season when he conceded 14 goals in six matches, and which included 4–1 defeats at Southampton and Derby County and a 3–0 setback at Manchester United. He claims that he was at fault with only three of those goals and that, even then, they were not major errors.

The first goal at Derby was scored by Gerry Daly, as a result of Shilton colliding with Larry Lloyd and dropping a cross to the Irish midfield player's feet. "The ball came in from the left," Shilton says, "and big Larry, who'd been marking a Derby forward on the other side started to move across to attack the ball as it came into the box. He came into the back of me and, in fact, had it been a Derby player, I think the referee would have given us a foul. But I'm not making excuses ... I should have shouted for the ball and besides, collision or no collision, I should still have held it."

Then there was Crystal Palace's goal, by Ian Walsh, in a 1–0 win over Forest two weeks later. Walsh, receiving a Vince Hilaire pass inside Frank Gray on the right flank, ran the full-back towards the goal-line, then checked, turned inside into the penalty area and from around eight yards mis-hit his shot not only through Gray's legs but Shilton's.

"I was covering the near post when Walsh took Frank towards the line and was shouting at Frank to make a tackle because I could see Walsh was shaping to cut inside and bend the ball to the far post with his left foot. Frank should really have tried to nail him at that stage as Walsh was running away from the goal. If Frank had been beaten by him, I could have come out to deal with Walsh. As it was, Frank was still a yard off Walsh when the Palace striker turned and, because he was just in front of me, I had to hang around on my goal-line, wondering what was going to happen next."

Finally, at Manchester United, the first of two goals Joe Jordan scored against Shilton that day came from a long kick by United's goalkeeper Gary Bailey. Jordan flicked the ball to Lou Macari and raced into the penalty area for the latter's first-time return. Shilton, thinking he had a chance of getting to the ball before Jordan, came out – but then hesitated when seeing two Forest defenders closing in on the striker, lost his footing on the frost-bound surface and Jordan, despite only getting a slight touch to the ball, managed to push it between Shilton's arms and legs.

When it comes, however, to the subject of managers publicly drawing attention to such mistakes Shilton becomes, if anything, even more animated. He reiterates his point about the tendency for 'keepers to be used as scapegoats, papering over the cracks created by other members of their teams and, indeed, the men in charge of them. "Goalkeepers need protection more than anything else," Shilton stresses. "I'm not saying that goalkeepers don't deserve to be criticised sometimes, because they do, but if a manager turns round and criticises a 'keeper for an *isolated* error, it's one of the worst things he can do."

A few minutes from the end of a Newcastle–Stoke match in 1975/76, with Stoke leading 1–0, Shilton's defenders pushed out too far and were caught hopelessly square by a ball played into the vast space behind them for Alan Gowling. Shilton raced more than 25 yards from his goal to reach the ball a split second or two before the Newcastle striker but it bounced awkwardly as he was about to boot it clear and then he completely mis-hit it. Shilton and Gowling collided ... and Gowling, no doubt motivated by the fact that he was closer to the ball, was first to his feet to push it into an open net. An embarrassing mistake, but Shilton says: "I could easily have stayed in my 18-yards box and let Gowling come at me with the ball. If I'd done that and he'd put it past me, most people would have

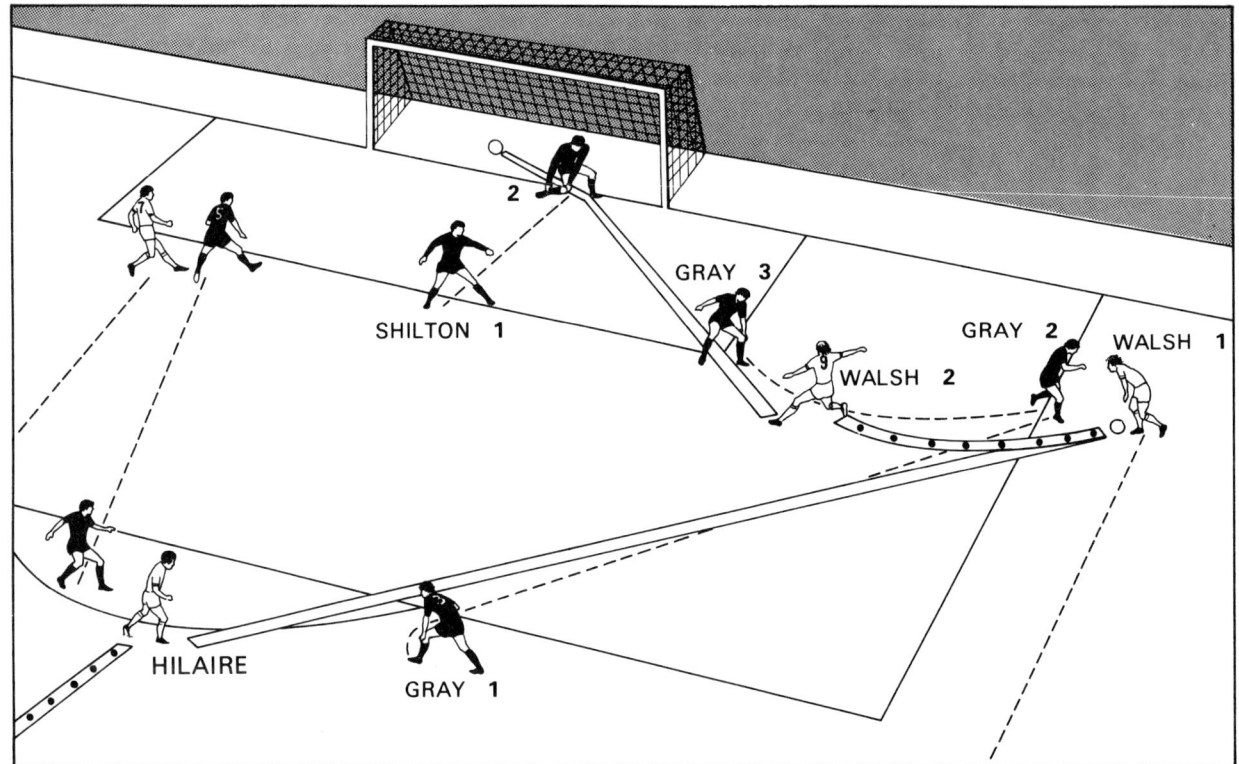

A Shilton error. Ian Walsh's goal in Crystal Palace's 1-0 win over Nottingham Forest in 1978.

Walsh, taking a pass from Vince Hilaire seemed too closely marked by Frank Gray to threaten Forest's goal. He still did, even when he checked, moved the ball inside, and onto his favourite left foot. With Gray continuing to concentrate on just blocking his path to goal,

Walsh hit a shot which not only went through Gray's legs but Shilton's as well.

"I was forced back onto my line because Frank was so close to me," Shilton says. "I was shouting at Frank to make a tackle as he was backing off Walsh, and when the shot came, I was late seeing the ball and was a little off-balance. The ball spun off my hands and hit the

inside of my leg before trickling into the net.

"Walsh wasn't in what you'd call a dangerous position when he gained possession, and I was looking to Frank to get in a tackle on him then. As it was, he kept backing off towards me and I had to hang around on my line wondering what was going to happen next."

---

blamed the defence for leaving so much space in front, but the fact that I tried to race him for the ball – the right decision – and lost out meant that I was the one who ultimately had to carry the can."

Stoke's manager Tony Waddington made no comment at all to Shilton afterwards, but it was a different story following another Newcastle–Stoke clash in 1976/77, the season Stoke were relegated. Then Shilton's failure to cut out a simple-looking cross ("He got too far under the ball and flicked at it," Waddington says) resulted in them losing 1–0.

"A schoolgirl could have saved that," Waddington told him.

Shilton accepted the criticism, partly because he himself felt the same way about the error and also because he appreciated the intense pressure on Waddington at that time. "What Tony Waddington said didn't affect me in any way," Shilton says, "but I don't agree with the basic principle of such remarks. If a goalkeeper isn't doing his job over a period of time, that's different, but if he is, then . . ."

The fact that goalkeepers' mistakes are inclined to stand out, to be spotlighted more than those of men filling outfield positions, focuses enormous attention on all the men filling the position and, as Shilton readily points out, some have been "destroyed" by it.

Such 'keepers include, for instance, Gary Sprake, the former Leeds United and Wales goalkeeper, who had the misfortune to make his occasional boobs in big matches, under the scrutiny of the TV cameras. His former manager, Don Revie, says Sprake lost his confidence as a result of such experiences and "became a bag of nerves on a big occasion." And another man with good reason to bemoan the way the mistakes of goalkeepers are magnified is Shilton's ex-Leicester teammate Carl Jayes, who had a spell with Northampton Town after leaving Leicester five years ago and is now in non-League football.

Jayes' potential was reflected in the fact that he made seven out of a possible eight appearances for England's schoolboy team one year. He was also in Leicester's reserves – as understudy to Shilton – when still at school studying for his A level exams. But Jayes had only a few first team games during his seven years with Leicester, and he partly attributes this to the psychological blow of a disastrous debut at the age of 18 – in a 2–0 FA Cup Fourth Round defeat by Orient at Filbert Street in 1972.

Jayes was told he'd be in the team an hour before the kick-off when Shilton, suffering from an injury, failed a late fitness test. "It would be wrong to say that I was nervous," Jayes insists. "I didn't have time to get nervous." He recalls that he did well for an hour or so, even though Orient gained a 1–0 lead, but then came the moment which he admits shattered him and which he claims caused Leicester's manager Jimmy Bloomfield – formerly Orient's manager – to "mistrust" him.

"It was one of those things that could happen to anybody," Jayes says. "Someone had the ball on the edge of our box and, with me moving to the far post expecting a long cross, he chipped it to the near post. I ran towards the ball and really it was so easy that I was actually thinking about where I was going to throw the ball before I'd even got it. Unfortunately, it went through my hands and by the time I'd got to it again it had gone just over the line."

Jayes made things worse by commenting to a reporter that, while he was to blame for the goal, he should not have been criticised because of the defeat. "As I walked to the dressing rooms, crying my eyes out, this fellow came up to me and asked how I felt. I didn't know who I was talking to – the state I was in it could have been Nat King Cole, anybody – and I blurted out something like: 'It wasn't my fault ... we wouldn't have scored from now until next week.' It made headlines and Bloomfield called me into his office and gave me a dressing-down about it.

"The gaffer didn't trust me after that match," Jayes says. "He actually used to say to me that he'd be quite prepared to put me in the first team for a few matches but that if he were to lose Peter Shilton permanently he would have to go out and get someone else. It didn't do my confidence much good."

Recalling the episode in his career, and the factors which caused him to accept his situation at Leicester for so long, Jayes agrees that he could have done with Shilton's self-confidence and strong personality. "I was a bit naive and allowed people to push me around," Jayes says. "The trouble is that I've always been the sort of lad who can't tread on people's toes. If someone punched me in the face today I'd probably be shaking hands with them tomorrow. Now Peter Shilton is exceptionally forceful and single-minded, isn't he?"

"I think you've got to be a bit philosophical," Shilton says. "You've got to accept that, like any human being, you're going to drop the odd clanger, do something really stupid from time to time. But this shouldn't bother you too much if you're a good goalkeeper. The difference between a good goalkeeper and a bad one is that the former makes the least number of mistakes."

Like Jayes, Shilton has himself experienced matches in which his team have bombarded the opposition for almost the entire 90 minutes without being able to get the ball in the net, only to be eventually sunk by a mistake by him at the other end. In these situations goalkeepers who admit to their mistakes – no matter how small these might have been – can sometimes find themselves facing all the brickbats alone. In Shilton's case, there is perhaps always a danger of that happening because he takes his determination to be honest – or rather to be seen to be honest – to the extreme. In any post-mortem he is likely to be the first man to hold up his hand in the dressing room to accept full responsibility for a defeat, even if he doesn't believe he has been totally to blame.

Shilton puts it this way: "Sometimes you can be too honest in football, too self-critical, because people tend to take things the wrong way. But I can't help the way I am made. It can be argued that no goal can be put down 100 per cent to the 'keeper. If the defenders in front of him are doing their jobs properly then he shouldn't need to make a save. But I find it very difficult to come out afterwards and say: 'Oh, I think I was *partly* to blame.' I prefer to

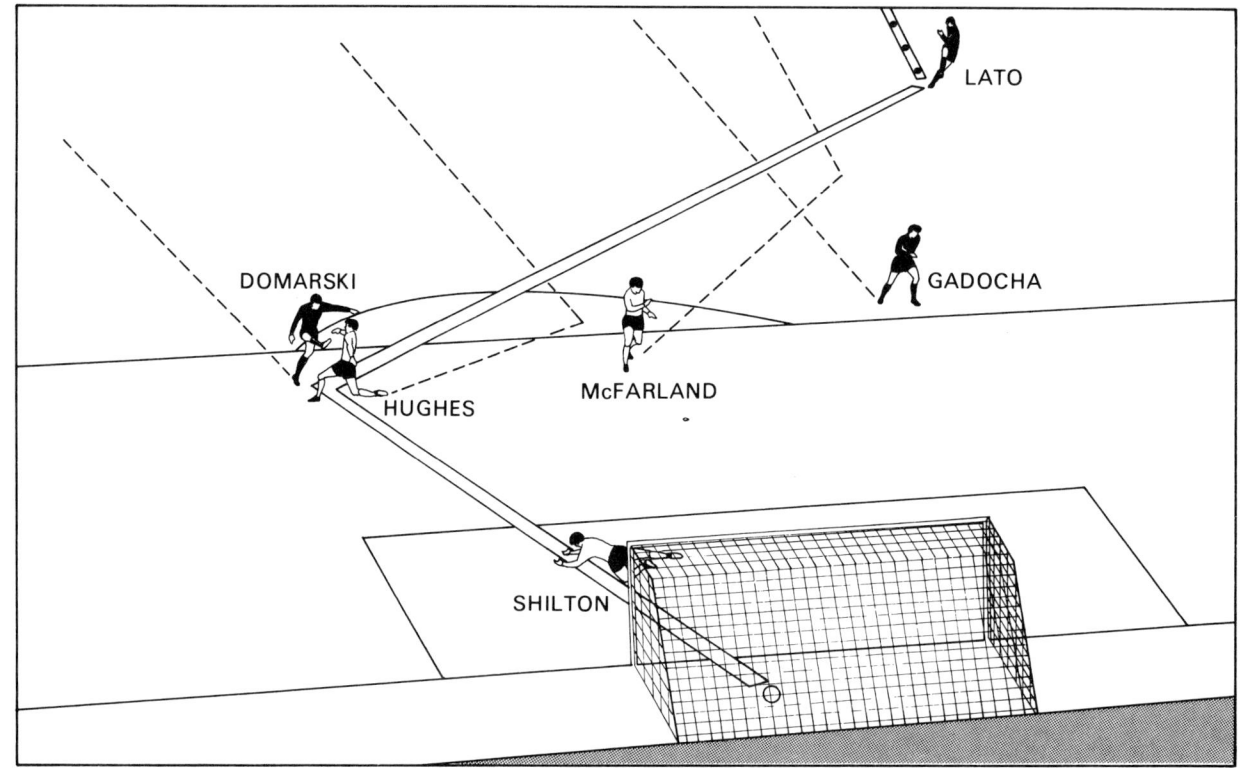

A Shilton error. The goal – by Anton Domarski – which gave Poland a 1-1 draw against England at Wembley in 1973, and knocked England out of the World Cup.

The England defence is opened up by a crossfield pass from Gregor Lato and Domarski, despite Emlyn Hughes's desperate attempt to get across to block the shot, manages to

hit the ball into the net through Hughes's legs, and under Shilton's diving body.

"We'd run the Poles ragged, without getting the ball in the net, and then suddenly this (top

be more direct, maybe to take all the blame and leave it to others to take a bit of the pressure off me by admitting where they might have gone wrong."

Such denigrating of himself rebounded heavily on Shilton following his "mistakes" in the England–Poland World Cup qualifying tie at Wembley in October 1973 and the Nottingham Forest–Wolves League Cup Final on the same ground in March 1980. They were errors which will forever loom large in the minds of those seeking to detract from his reputation as the best goalkeeper in the world, but the slight dents to his image were in fact self-inflicted to a great extent due to Shilton's unwillingness to publicly reveal what he really felt about the goals he conceded in those important matches. Even so, his experiences of attracting more criticism than he deserved goes a long way towards explaining his almost bitter, chip-on-the-shoulder attitude towards the way goalkeepers are regarded.

England, World Cup winners in 1966 and quarter-finalists in 1970, needed to win on that damp night in October to clinch a place in the final stages of the 1974 competition at Poland's expense. An indication of the pattern of that game is that, in the physical sense, Shilton spent virtually the entire 90 minutes as little more than a spectator. But, on one of the few occasions that the Poles got as far as England's penalty area, Shilton was beaten by a low Anton Domarski shot, to his left, which went under his diving body. Allan Clarke later made it 1-1 from a penalty, but the Poles held on under almost unbearable pressure, to knock England out of the competition and ultimately their manager Alf Ramsey out of a job.

Shilton feels he should have saved Domarski's shot. He does so even taking into account that Domarski – who'd run onto a cross-field Gregor Lato pass, just inside England's penalty area on the

right)...it happened so quickly and really the look of bewilderment on the England players' faces said it all.

"It wasn't an easy shot for me to deal with because, apart from the fact that Domarski struck the ball exceptionally well, the Wembley pitch that night was very greasy and I was a bit unsighted by Emlyn.

"Unfortunately, I made the mistake of trying to make the perfect save. In that sort of situation, I should have concentrated just on getting to the ball, knocking it behind for a corner or something like that. But I attempted to hold it by scooping it into my body, and the pace beat me."

right – hit the ball well on a slippery surface; and that Shilton was unsighted by Emlyn Hughes's desperate attempt to block the shot.

"It happened so quickly," Shilton recalls. "The ball seemed to fly past me and was in the net before I knew what had happened. It was a difficult situation but I had to accept responsibility as I tried to make the *perfect* save. The ball went quite close to my feet. I attempted to sort of scoop it into my body. In that situation, I think I should have forgotten about holding the ball and just tried to stop it."

Be that as it may, Hunter can be said to have been equally to blame for the goal. He missed a tackle on Lato at the start of the move which led up to Domarski's stunning finish. There seemed little danger to England when Lato gained possession on the left, around the half-way line. Then Hunter, who had Lato trapped on the touchline, gave the Pole an escape route when he committed himself. Lato surged forward, drawing other defenders towards him, before finding the unmarked Domarski with the decisive pass.

And in Shilton's defence there remains the inability of England to convert their numerous scoring chances. Poland's goalkeeper, Jan Tomaszewski, was ungraciously described by Brian Clough on TV as a "clown", as he repeatedly kept out shots and headers seemingly more by accident than design, and had the game of his life. Tomaszewski suddenly gained a status in the game, perhaps above his true ability, but England had only themselves to blame. As Shilton says: "With any reasonable amount of luck, we'd have won something like 6–1."

A similar tale unfolded when Nottingham Forest met Wolves in the 1980 League Cup Final, hot favourites to win the competition for a record third

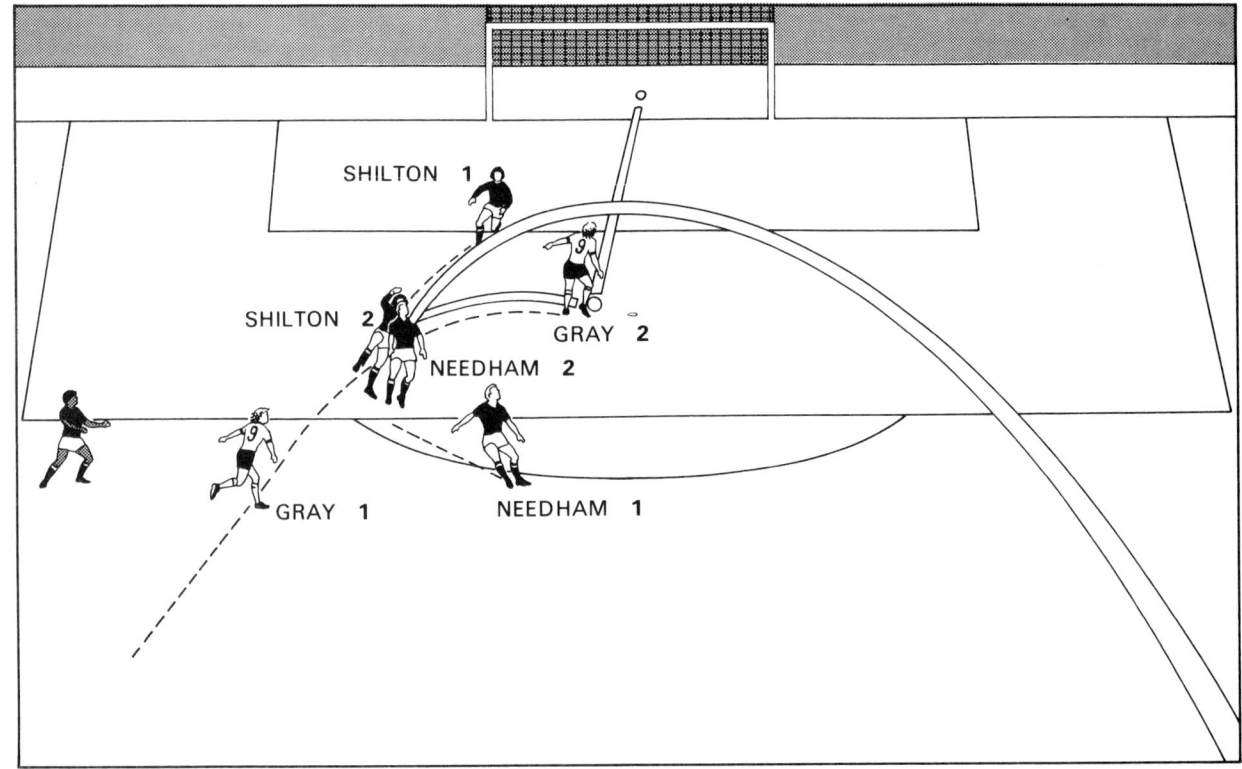

A Shilton error. Andy Gray's goal (above and right) in Wolves's 1-0 win over Nottingham Forest in the 1980 League Cup Final.

Forest's centre-half David Needham moved backwards to get to a long high ball from Wolves's full-back Geoff Palmer as Shilton, in the belief it was going to go over his head, came out to take command of the situation. But Needham got his chest to the ball as Shilton approached him, the two men collided, and Gray – the man for whom Palmer's speculative pass had been intended – was presented with the easiest of scoring chances.

"On reflection, I think that season in succession. Despite Forest's overall domination of the match, Wolves won 1-0 with a simple goal by Andy Gray following an extraordinary mix-up involving Shilton and centre-half David Needham. After the game Shilton went on record as saying he was to blame for the goal and Brian Clough (while pointing out that Forest's forwards, who had missed some good chances, had to carry much of the responsibility) echoed the comment.

In the dressing room, Clough had asked Shilton: "Peter, who was to blame for that goal?"

"I was," Shilton replied.

"Good," Clough said. "It *was* you, not David Needham, and I'm pleased we've got that established now."

Clough expresses surprise when you suggest to him now that it wasn't totally Shilton's fault. "I think it was," he says. "It was *totally* his fault because Peter Shilton could see everything. Dave Needham didn't know where he was, where Peter was."

The ball which caught Shilton and Needham in difficulties came from Wolves full-back Geoff Palmer. Gaining possession on the right-hand side of the field, just inside his own half, Palmer attempted to find Gray on the left with a long cross aimed over Needham and into the space behind him on the edge of Forest's penalty area. "For a moment," Shilton recalls, "I thought the ball was going to clear David and started coming out to make sure that if he couldn't get it, I would." Suddenly though, the ball dipped and Shilton, within six yards of Needham, who was running backwards, gave him a sort of half-hearted shout to let him know where he was. Needham seemed to chest the ball down, (expecting Shilton to collect it, he said later) but in the next split second, Gray was onto it, and Shilton and

maybe I shouldn't have come for that ball," Shilton says. "If I hadn't, and Gray had beaten David and put it in the net, everyone would probably have blamed David. The thing was, I was trying to be positive and, on this occasion, it rebounded on me.

"It seemed to me that the ball was going to beat David and I thought: 'Well, if it goes over his head, you've got to make sure Gray doesn't get it.' However, the flight of the Football League ball does tend to be unpredictable. In this particular instance, it suddenly just seemed to stop in mid-air."

Needham collided to give the Scotland centre-forward an open goal.

Shilton is always reticent about pinpointing where others might have been responsible for the "bad goals" he has conceded, but never more so than when recalling this last incident. "There's no way I want to shift the blame onto someone else," he stresses. "You're either to blame or you're not to blame and in this particular case, I was to blame because I came off my line and never got the ball. I should have perhaps stayed where I was and waited for the situation to develop a little bit more."

However, when pushed, Shilton presents another side to the story.

"The day after the League Cup Final, the missus had a go at me over what I'd said about the goal in the newspapers," Shilton says. "She's extremely honest with me. If I think I was to blame for a goal, she won't say: 'Oh, you were diabolical' or anything like that, but she won't give me any bull either. Anyway, she was looking through the newspapers, at the reports of the match, and just turned to me and said: 'I think you're an idiot for making comments like that.' I explained why it was partly my fault and why I had to admit to it, and she said: 'Well, that may be so but why take all the blame on your shoulders? What was David Needham doing?'

"I just think David got caught in two minds a little bit. He suspected I was coming up behind him, but wasn't quite sure where I was and in the end he more or less let the ball hit him instead of adopting a positive attitude and getting it away. Even in the best organised defences, there are times when you and one of the centre-backs will be going for the same ball, neither of you sure whose ball it is and it's essential that the man nearest to the ball takes the initiative. That's what I felt David should have done in that situation."

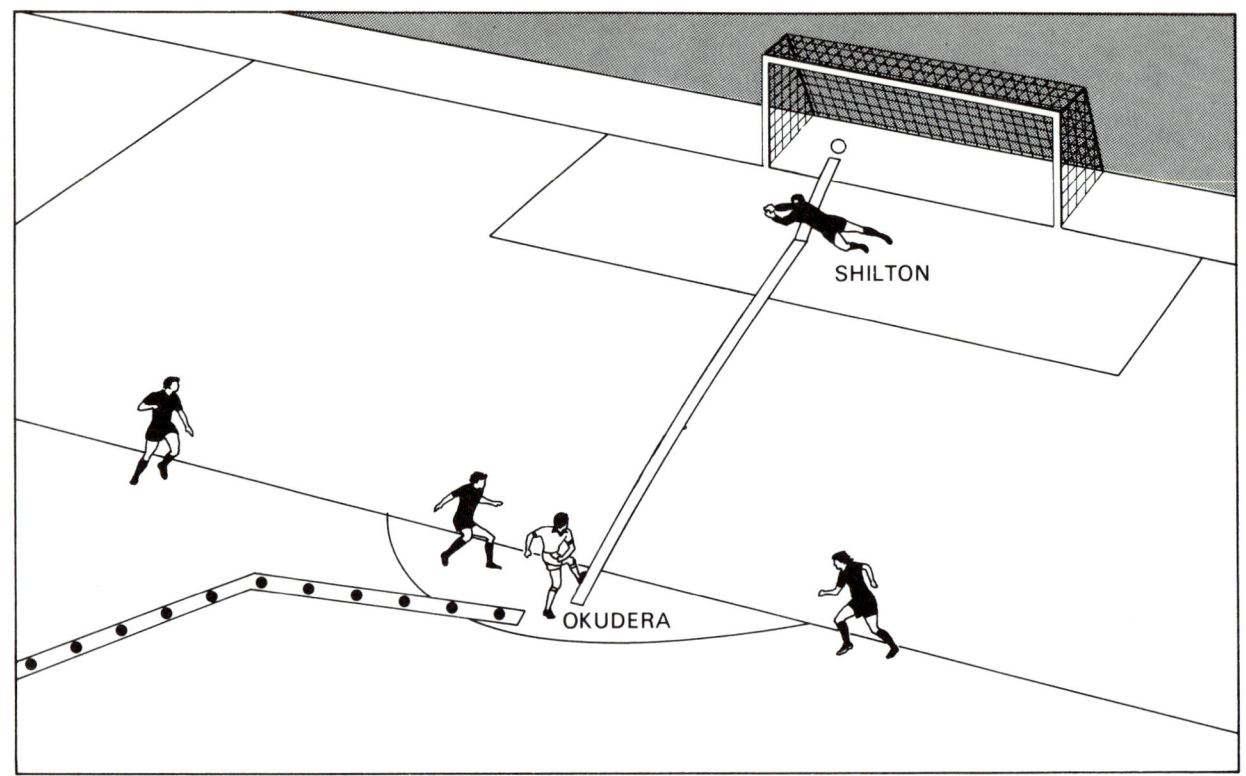

A Shilton error. The goal, by Cologne's Japanese substitute Yasuhiko Okudera which gave the West German team a 3-3 draw in the first leg of the European Cup semi-final tie in 1979, at Forest.

Forest, 0-2 behind at one stage, were leading 3-2 when Okudera hit a tame-looking shot from outside the penalty area. Shilton seemed to have it well covered but the ball went under his outstretched arms, and into the net.

"Oh, I did feel pretty sick about that one," he recalls, grimacing. "Fortunately, Forest won the second leg 1-0 but if the result had gone the other way, the memory of that mistake would have haunted me for the rest of my life."

Shilton considers that the mistake can be partly attributed to the fact that he spent too long the previous day in a shot-stopping training session, with Forest teammates Tony Woodcock and David Needham, in conditions which varied considerably to those he experienced against Cologne. "In that training session," he explains, "the ball rose much more sharply after hitting the ground than it did in the Cologne match.

"I was anticipating the shot from Okudera to come at me higher than it did, and took my eyes off the ball."

Needham, who played with Shilton in the Leicester schoolboys representative team, was included in Forest's side for that match because their regular centre-half, Larry Lloyd, was suspended. Nevertheless Shilton disagrees that the goal stemmed from their comparatively limited experience of operating together. "No, we'd had a good understanding on the previous occasion we'd played together," Shilton says.

Looking back, Shilton sees the period as one of the most depressing of his career. Three days before their League Cup Final defeat by Wolves, Forest – then European Cup holders – had been beaten 1-0 in their first leg quarter-final against Dynamo Berlin. But the depression was quickly put to flight the following week when Forest, inspired by Shilton, picked themselves off the floor to beat Dynamo 3-1 in the return leg in East Germany. It was a particularly sweet moment for Shilton, who has always prided himself on being able to recover from set-backs. "They do affect you," he says, "but there comes a point when my stomach just tightens. I am determined to come fighting back. For me, that's the true test of a player – how he reacts to things going against him. What delighted me most of all about our match in Berlin was not just my own performance but the confidence that our defence had in me."

There was a similar show of defiance from Shilton in the 1978/79 European Cup, when Forest were held 3–3 by Cologne in the first leg semi-final at the City Ground, and then produced the major surprise of that season's competition by winning the second leg 1–0. In the first match, Forest had fought back from 0–2 to 3–2, only for Shilton to present the Germans with their equaliser near the end, through probably the most glaring bloomer of his career.

The goal came from Cologne's substitute, a tricky Japanese winger called Yasuhiko Okudera, with a tame-looking shot to Shilton's right from outside the penalty area. Shilton had it covered so well he would probably have held it with one eye closed in normal circumstances. But the ball, bouncing before reaching Shilton, came at him lower than he'd anticipated and went under his outstretched arms.

Shilton thinks the error stemmed partly from the fact that he'd spent some time the day before the match dealing with shots from outside the box delivered by David Needham and Tony Woodcock. This was to accommodate a photographer who wanted pictures for a football annual of him in training. The conditions varied considerably to those Shilton experienced against Cologne. Shilton explains: "There was a hell of a lot of water on the pitch during that training session. I found that when the ball bounced, it rose quite sharply. But the pitch had dried out and was more tacky on the night of the match and shots were keeping lower."

Shilton, who has since made a point of not doing too much of that type of training the day before a match, also blamed himself for Cologne's first goal, from Roger Van Gool. It was a low shot which went over his hands and into the net, bouncing off each upright.

There have been, inevitably, other Shilton bloomers in an English League career spanning more than 15 years. But the total of goals for which he has been responsible is ridiculously small compared with the number of goals he has saved. The proof of that resides in the in-depth dossiers kept by many clubs on the strengths and weaknesses of footballers liable to oppose them, or whom they might want to buy, and it's fair to say that there aren't many words in the "weaknesses" sections of these dossiers as far as Shilton is concerned. Such is the case, that opposing teams sometimes try to invent a Shilton flaw to boost their confidence.

Leicester's Mark Wallington is fond of relating the amusing story of a match against Stoke, when centre-forward Frank Worthington told anyone prepared to listen that Shilton was "suspect" to shots on his left side. "Frank actually got a goal with such a shot in that match," Wallington recalls. "The ball went in like a rocket – no goalkeeper in the world would have stopped it – and afterwards Frank came into the dressing room with a big grin on his face and said: 'There you are . . . I told you Shilts is vulnerable to shots to his left.'"

Shilton has faced all of Britain's outstanding strikers (and a fair number outside Britain, too) since making his Leicester debut in the mid-Sixties. None of these strikers has scored enough times against him to cause him any loss of sleep on the eve of his matches against them. Over the past 10 years, the striker with the best scoring record against Shilton (without needing the help of penalties) has been John Toshack, the former Liverpool and Wales centre-forward, who put a total of seven goals past him in the days that he operated at Liverpool alongside Kevin Keegan. Toshack is followed by Peter Osgood, Bob Latchford, Brian "Pop" Robson (5); and Peter Lorimer, Ian Wallace, Kenny Burns, Chris Garland, John Hickton, Geoff Hurst, George Telfer, Billy Jennings, Kevin Keegan, Brian Kidd, David Mills, John Richards and Frank Worthington (4). Only four players have got hat-tricks against him during this period: Kenny Burns, Ian Wallace (both of whom have since become his teammates at Nottingham Forest), Bob Latchford and Billy Jennings.

The greatest goal he's ever had scored against him, he says, was a dazzling Jimmy Greaves effort for Tottenham against Leicester at White Hart Lane in the late 1960's. It started with a long, high ball towards the right touchline from Tottenham's 'keeper Pat Jennings, which Greaves just managed to keep in play. Almost in the same moment, Greaves dummied past one Leicester defender, dribbled past three more in an extraordinary diagonal run into the penalty area, and finally went around Shilton also before slipping the ball into the empty net. It was a goal which summed up Greaves's tremendous technical skills, pace, coolness and confidence and, as Shilton recalls, the crowd were still applauding him as Leicester re-started the match.

Of the other "big name" strikers of the past, Shilton also had a great admiration for Denis Law ("because of his sharp reflexes and courage inside the box") and his old Leicester City teammate Allan Clarke.

GREAVES
1
2
3
4
5
6

Jimmy Greaves (extreme right, opposite page), was not only the greatest British goalscorer of all time but the man who, according to Shilton, got the best-ever goal against him, in a Tottenham–Leicester City match at White Hart Lane.

Shilton recalls that it was so spectacular that the crowd were still applauding it as his stunned Leicester teammates re-started the match. Greaves, gaining possession on the right wing from a long kick by goal-keeper Pat Jennings ("He did great just to keep the ball in play," Shilton recalls) beat a Leicester defender on the turn and went past at least two more in an extraordinary diagonal

Shilton has always felt something of an affinity with Clarke, as Clarke, too, possesses a single-mindedness that can sometimes be interpreted as ruthlessness and selfishness. Shilton recalls the time when he and Clarke were looked upon as the stars of the Leicester team which reached the FA Cup Final in 1969. Both felt that because they were so much in demand for newspaper interviews, personal appearances and so forth, they should be allowed to divorce themselves from the other players when it came to contributing their income from these sources to the team's "perks pool". Eventually Shilton relented but Clarke remained adamant on the issue and went his own way. "I felt he was wrong, to be honest," Shilton says, "but there's no way I could condemn him for that attitude because it's one of the reasons why he was such a fabulous finisher. He's very positive in everything he does and, while he's not always right, this is something which I cannot help but admire."

Shilton rates Clarke's scoring ability almost as high as he does Greaves's. "Greaves was the best of the lot, and certainly in a class of his own in being able to dribble around people, as if they weren't there, to create his own chances, but when it came to actually finishing I'd say Allan was definitely on a par with him.

"Like all the great strikers Allan was too arrogant, too confident in his own ability ever to think too much about the man he was trying to beat. When we had shooting practice at Leicester there were days when I felt almost unbeatable, but Clarkey was probably the only player there who would never be psyched by me. He'd be coming through with the ball and as he hit it, he'd look up as if to say: 'You bloody save that one then.' He could read situations and react to them so quickly. That's the hallmark of all outstanding footballers. What separates them

run into Shilton's penalty area. Shilton came off his line but Greaves left him, too, on his backside before slipping the ball into an empty net.

"He was just taking on everyone who came to him," Shilton says. "You could never be sure what the guy was going to do because he was a football genius. One of the great things about him was his coolness – he had only me to beat 12–15 yards from goal, and in that position, I'd have been expecting a shot from most players.

"But no, Greaves, continuing to come at me with the ball, swivelled his hips to get me going one way, and went the other."

---

from the rest is that they always seem to have that extra bit of time to do whatever they want with the ball."

Listening to Shilton one gains an insight into the nightmare Clarke presented to goalkeepers. He knew, intuitively, what the men in this position were thinking and attempting to do in certain situations. He could nearly always be relied upon to give them the most difficult of saves to make. "He was tremendous at that," Shilton enthuses. "If he got a square ball in the box, then you could bet that he'd hit his shot a fraction early so as to catch the 'keeper while he was moving into position and wasn't properly balanced.

"Allan was an excellent striker of the ball, and even if the goalkeeper was in the right position, he was always liable to chip the ball over his head or bend it around him, whereas a lot of strikers would have just hit it and hoped."

When assessing strikers Shilton inevitably looks for a similar positive and aggressive attitude to the one he likes to think he possesses himself. It explains why he is enthusiastic about the young, up-and-coming First Division strikers of today, such as Justin Fashanu and Cyrille Regis.

When Shilton first played against Fashanu at Norwich during the 1979/80 season, he was immediately impressed by his strength, athleticism and refusal to allow himself to be intimidated physically. "Early in the match," Shilton recalls, "Larry Lloyd and Ken Burns got in some really heavy tackles on him, to sort of test him out, and he was quite willing to battle them."

Shilton says that Regis, while possessing all the technical ability he looks for in a striker, once gave him the impression of being lazy. "But," Shilton adds, "he has matured a lot in the last year or two. What I particularly like about him is that he doesn't allow defenders to dictate to him. It irritates me sometimes to see strikers coming off their markers, as the ball is about to be played up to them, because it can lead to them going too deep. If a forward moves a yard off his marker, the next time he might be pushed back two yards, then three yards and so on. In this situation, Regis will back onto his marker – he'll always be looking to go forward.''

Shilton is as critical of other players as he is of himself, goal-scorers especially, because he can so easily relate to the problems such men face and the pressure they experience in doing ''the second most important job in football.''

An indication of the standards Shilton will expect from his strikers, when and if he becomes a manager, was provided by comments he once made about Trevor Francis. It was not long after Francis's record £1 million transfer from Birmingham to Nottingham Forest. The comments – in a weekly newspaper column by Shilton – were generally flattering but Shilton felt obliged to make the point that Francis needed to ''broaden his outlook'' on the game. ''He's suffered through being labelled a Superstar,'' Shilton said. ''He hasn't done enough in the game yet to justify that sort of reputation and it has led to him becoming too much of an individualist, a bit too narrow-minded in the footballing sense.'' A fan of Francis sent him a clipping of the article – which, unfortunately had been cut so that the tone of it was distorted – and a short note to the effect: ''Is Peter Shilton a friend of yours?'' Francis challenged Shilton about his criticism of him, but was appeased when shown the un-edited version of the article and given a fuller explanation of the point Shilton was trying to get across.

Shilton, who feels that Francis has been helped greatly at Forest through being used in different roles – wide on the right or in midfield – likens him to Karl Heinz Rummenigge, the outstanding Bayern Munich and West Germany forward. ''Like Rummenigge he has explosive pace,'' Shilton points out, ''but Trevor has tighter ball control and there is more variation to his game.'' When you ask him to name the other present-day strikers he most admires, the first men he mentions are Ken Dalglish, Andy Gray and Kevin Keegan. He has this to say about each:

Allan Clarke (right), the former Leicester, Leeds and England striker who ranks almost as high as Greaves on Shilton's list of outstanding English League strikers of the past. "He could nearly always be relied upon to give goalkeepers the most difficult of saves to make."

Dalglish: "Like Allan Clarke he's very good at curling balls around you. He can so easily fool you. He'll be running towards the edge of the box with a defender in front and then, as you're moving to the edge of your six-yards box, he's liable to hit it early without first going past his marker. He's at his most dangerous when the ball is played up to him in or around the box and he has his back to the goal. This is because, apart from his ability to turn people, he's probably the best shielder of a ball in the game. It's difficult for a goalkeeper since instead of turning and getting in a shot (A) Dalglish will hold, and hold and hold – then suddenly force you to change your position by laying the ball square for someone else to have a crack (B). It's why Liverpool's midfield players get so many goals. This is one of the reasons why Dalglish is held in such high esteem among English League managers, coaches and players.

"Unlike a number of other strikers, he uses his ability in the best interests of his team and you can always rely upon him giving 100 per cent. Although no-one can deny that Dalglish is a genuine international-class footballer, it's fair to say that he hasn't generally played as well for Scotland as he has for Liverpool. The only explanation I can give is that Liverpool seem to use him more as a target man than Scotland – in some of the Scotland matches I have seen, someone like Joe Jordan or Andy Gray has been filling that role, with Dalglish feeding off him.

"As with all outstanding goalscorers, Dalglish has the magic knack of being in the right place at the right time, and is an excellent striker of the ball. Most of my best saves against him have been from shots from just inside or outside the 18-yard box. I have a good record against him actually – the only goal I can remember him scoring against me was in Liverpool's 2-0 FA Cup fourth round win over Nottingham Forest in 1980. I failed to hold a high, curling ball from Phil Neal and Dalglish was there to bang it in.

"However, as I said, he's more than a goal scorer. Of all the strikers I play against, I'd say he is the best in terms of all-round ability."

99

Gray: "He's what you'd call an old-fashioned type centre-forward: he's not the most skilful of players, not a Greaves or a Clarke, but he never stops running and probably attacks balls in the box with greater determination and aggression than any other No. 9 I can think of, with the possible exception of Joe Jordan. He's so brave, the sort of player who will go in where it really hurts and turn what seem bad balls for him into good balls. He's particularly dangerous in the air, of course, and to be honest, if Gray's around when I'm challenging for a high ball, then nine times out of ten I'll be quite happy to punch it out rather than catch it. He creates problems just through his attitude . . . if a high ball is played into a group of defenders, and it's maybe 60–40 in their favour, you'll suddenly see Gray coming late and just getting a foot or half a yard on the man about to clear the ball. He creates chances out of nothing.

"This diagram sums him up to a T. He's come from nowhere to get his head to the ball, and he's either going to stick it in the net or give someone else the chance to do so. The opposing defence have been taken by surprise, and the onus is on the goalkeeper to perform a miracle to get them out of trouble.

"Having said that, I think it's important that Gray is given the right sort of service. There's no point in teams with men like him repeatedly trying to 'hit' them with high balls into the box from deep positions because, with their backs to the goal, it's virtually impossible for them to score. They need wingers who can get around the back of a defence and produce crosses from on or near the goal-line.

"It's significant that virtually all the No. 9s in Gray's mould have been at their most effective when playing with orthodox wingers.

"For example Peter Withe, Villa's top scorer last season when they won the Championship, would be the first to admit that he relied heavily on Tony Morley. "It's a pity that Wolves (who bought Gray from Villa for £1·4 million) haven't had a Morley to bring the best out of him.""

Keegan: "A tremendous little finisher, he makes it hard for goalkeepers to read his shots because he hits the ball so quickly. He doesn't need to wind himself up to get maximum power. Another outstanding feature of Kevin's game is the way he creates shooting chances for himself – he's great at turning people and at playing little one-twos with people in or around the box. Remember the way he combined with Trevor Brooking to score that magnificent goal in England's 3–1 win over Scotland at Wembley in 1979? And another thing you've got to watch out for are his runs on the blind side of defenders. When he's around it's fatal to have defenders watching the ball rather than where opponents are running to off it. That is what is happening in the illustration below. Keegan has made a typical blind-side run and, with the ball being headed into his path on the edge of the 18-yard box, the onus is suddenly on the goalkeeper to get his defence out of trouble.

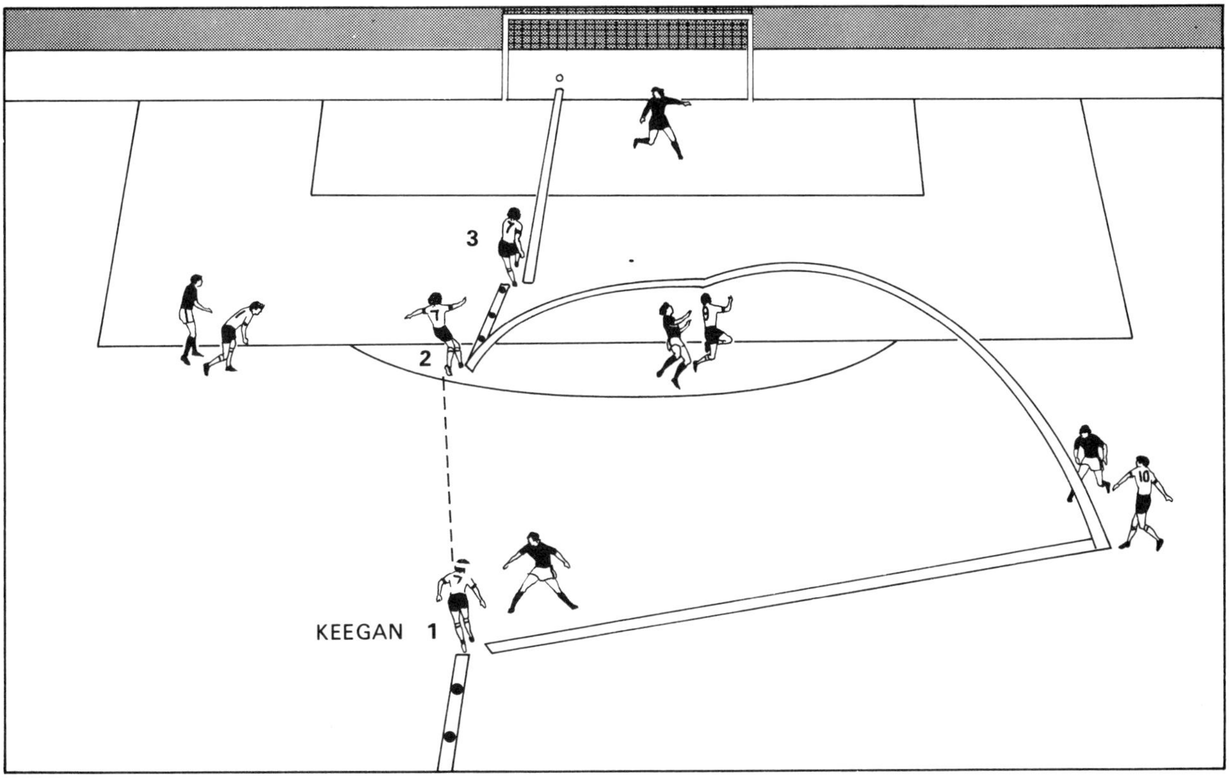

"The goalkeeper is on a hiding to nothing because, apart from his problem in quickly switching his attention to Keegan, and changing direction, Keegan is very positive and decisive in these situations – he knows exactly what he's got to do and you can be sure that he'll do it with the minimum fuss and bother.

"I well remember his goal against me when Liverpool beat Leicester 3-1 in an FA Cup semi-final replay at Villa Park in 1974 – it was a Keegan classic. There was a long ball through the middle and Keegan, while running forward, let it drop over his shoulder and then hit it first-time on the volley. I'm hard-pressed to think of any First Division striker who in that situation would have hit the ball as early as Keegan did.

"I wore an all-white strip in those days and after the Liverpool game, Jimmy Hill suggested on TV that it had made it easy for Kevin to see where I was positioned.

"In fact, when I later discussed this point with Kevin, he said that he didn't actually see me until after he'd struck the shot. It was an instinctive goal."

7

WHY RAY'S NO LAUGH

Shilton and Ray Clemence promoting the record they made together in 1980. Its title was, appropriately "Side by Side".

Despite his superstar status in British football there are times when Peter Shilton, frustrated by unrealised ambitions, seems lost in a cloud of gloom and despondency. Nothing is liable to drive him into one of those black spells more quickly than the subject of his rivalry with Ray Clemence in the England squad.

It's not difficult to appreciate why Shilton is so sensitive about the rivalry. He desperately wants to be regarded not only as the best goalkeeper in Britain, or the world, but *seen* to be the best. Although a large number of professionals acknowledge him in that light, Shilton knows that the assessment can never be taken seriously if he's not officially the No. 1 goalkeeper in the England squad. The fact is that Clemence has denied him such status for a long time, and made considerably more international appearances. It is a sore point with Shilton, to put it mildly.

Both are great goalkeepers. Most people in the game consider that there's little to choose between them. It's why Ron Greenwood, no doubt mindful of the blow to Shilton's pride through having to accept second-billing to Clemence in the England side, has decided to use them in alternate matches, operating in effect a sort of rota for the goalkeeper's spot. Indeed, on one occasion – the 4–3 defeat by Austria in Vienna in June 1979 – Greenwood selected Shilton for the first half and Clemence for the second.

While such a policy would seem to be the perfect solution to this most difficult of selection problems, it has only partly eased Shilton's frustration.

"I don't like talking about Ray Clemence and myself because the more I talk about us the more it seems to pull us together," Shilton says. "We are looked upon similarly and that really bugs me because I don't think we are the same. No two people can be exactly alike – one must be better than the other. Although I've never discussed it with him, I sense that he doesn't feel as strongly about it as I do. I can be selfish – I openly admit it – but I can't help it. I just don't like being looked upon as the same as someone else and, if necessary, I'll be striving to prove myself better than anyone else to the end of my days."

Clemence, more than a year older than Shilton and, at 5ft 11½in and 12st 9lb, fractionally smaller, is certainly different to Shilton in temperament and personality. As Shilton suggests, Clemence, a genuinely modest, even self-effacing man, is the more relaxed and easy-going of the two.

"Peter's the more dominant personality," Larry Lloyd says. "Not as easy to get on with as Ray, to be honest ... with his definite views on goalkeeping, and about most things.

Clemence, who regards goalkeeping as one of life's gifts, an art which can be improved but not created by endeavour, has reached parity partly through fate. Born and raised in the seaside town of Skegness, Clemence played much of his schoolboy football at left-half. He never wanted to be a goalkeeper, and after leaving school he combined accountancy studies with a job as a deckchair attendant. He got the chance to enter professional football at 16 when, persuaded to go in goal for his youth team in a cup final, he was spotted by a Scunthorpe scout and signed by them as an apprentice.

When Clemence was in Scunthorpe's 'A' team he was so depressed by a run of heavy defeats he nearly quit the game. But one of the Scunthorpe coaches encouraged him to stick with the game. He told Clemence he should have more confidence in himself. "Look, you've got the ability," he said, "but you need to give yourself a kick up the backside."

Three years later, at the age of 19, Clemence was bought by Liverpool for £20,000 ... and, after two frustrating seasons as understudy to Tommy Lawrence, established himself as a first-team regular. Clemence spent 14 years at Liverpool before his £300,000 transfer to Tottenham in August 1981.

Shilton's greater self-confidence means he is inclined to be more assertive than Clemence on the field and therefore more influential. To a great extent, Shilton's teams adapt their style of play in defence to suit his attributes and qualities. With Clemence it has been the other way around.

"Liverpool pushed back onto Ray Clemence when opposing teams were putting them under pressure and gave him comparatively little space to come out for crosses," Gordon Banks explains. "But Peter Shilton has always wanted that area immediately in front of him free. He's great on crosses and if the opposition have the ball in a wide position, and he can see they're going to hit it into the middle, he'll immediately push his defenders out to give himself room to take it."

Shilton nods in agreement. "Liverpool have tended to protect their goalkeepers in this way for as long as I can remember," he says. "When Tommy Lawrence was in goal for them, I often used to see big Ron Yeats heading balls away from the edge of the six-yards box, and I notice Phil Thompson and Alan Hansen doing the same today."

As Shilton points out, Liverpool generally like to push up on teams when they are in possession. It means that if they lose the ball their opponents find it difficult to launch an effective counter-attack without being caught offside. One of the reasons why Liverpool's offside trap worked so effectively when Clemence was in the side is that on the rare occasions it was beaten, Clemence could nearly always be relied upon to come out of his 18-yards box to get to the ball before the man for whom the pass had been intended. He acted like a sweeper.

Shilton, however, is irritated by the suggestion that Clemence is superior in this department. "I've had plenty of these situations at Nottingham Forest.

Clemence – Shilton's strongest competitor. "We get extremely close sometimes," Shilton says of his friend and rival, "but there's still that barrier and it will probably always be there."

The ball has been hit through or over our defence on the half-way line and the odds have been 60–40 or 70–30 against me getting to it first," he says. "When that happens, the only difference between me and Ray is that I'll be more inclined to hold back – to try and psyche the other man out." This approach, he says, is a safeguard against him not reaching the ball (and being lobbed), or bringing his opponent down, and conceding a free kick.

Shilton is reticent about discussing his rivalry with Clemence – at least with outsiders. He feels he cannot trust himself to be diplomatic, or avoid saying what he really believes. There is a danger, also, of not expressing his thoughts with sufficient lucidity and being misconstrued. "I just can't win," Shilton says.

There was a good example of how delicate this subject has become to Shilton when Ron Greenwood selected Clemence for England's opening match in the 1980 European Nations Cup Final against Belgium in Italy. It created something of a surprise because it was Shilton's "turn" to play. Clemence had appeared in the previous match against Scotland and Shilton, who had helped Nottingham Forest win the European Cup with his dazzling display against Hamburg, was regarded as the goalkeeper in the best form. Bitterly upset at being left out he found it difficult to hide his feelings when interviewed by a newspaper reporter on the subject.

"Naturally I am very disappointed," he told him, "but as far as I am concerned, I'm just a member of a squad and I wish Ray all the best."

When seeing the way the newspapers treated the story the following day Shilton was concerned that his comments might have given the impression of disharmony in the England squad. He therefore brought the subject up at a team meeting, reiterating what he'd said to the media and how he had said it.

Ipswich's Mick Mills recounted a similar experience and the meeting was concluding with Emlyn Hughes, one of the senior members of the squad, stressing the importance of the players not allowing anything which appeared in the media to affect their spirit of cameraderie, when England's captain Kevin Keegan added: "In any case Peter has apologised for what's happened."

"No, Kevin," Shilton corrected him. "I've not *apologised* because I haven't done anything to apologise for."

There is a the thin dividing line in the relationship of Shilton and Clemence – the difference between being colleagues and fierce rivals – and it is important to Shilton that it's not crossed either way. Although they get on well, Shilton is forever conscious of "that barrier between us", as for example during the 1980 European Nations' Cup Finals. Then, after Shilton had been left out of the team for England's opening match, Ron Greenwood sprung an equally big surprise by including him in the side for the next game, against Italy.

It was looked upon as England's most important match of the competition and Shilton recalls: "I was a bit surprised at Ray's reaction – it was the first time I'd ever seen him a little narked. I mean he tried not to show it, but I could tell he was upset as soon as he came into the room."

According to Shilton, he and Clemence have never ever discussed their rivalry, nor the ways in which they differ as goalkeepers. "We watch each other in training," Shilton says, "and whereas we might make general observations about each other, neither of us commits himself too much, or gets too involved. It's like a sort of unwritten law really ... I mean, we both know our jobs. He knows what he's good at, I know what I'm good at, so there's nothing to discuss.

"Sometimes, we'll drift away from each other, and other times we'll get extremely cross. But if we go out anywhere, we usually stick together. One day, for example, we went to the races at Newbury with some of the other England lads, and we had a tremendous time together, cheering the winners home and what have you. He's not a racing man but somehow he mucked in with me and really got into it.

"But there's still that barrier and it will probably always be there."

It can be argued that there's more than one way to do a job, that Shilton's aggressive, dominating approach to the game has been less important to the England team than to his Football League sides, particularly since in international football he is operating with so many other top-class, accomplished men. But Shilton disputes this and it is a measure of the man that he does. "More than one way to do the job?" he asks, incredulously. "No there's not. There's only one way – the right way.

"There are a lot of good English League footballers who seem to get completely lost when they are brought into an international team," he says. "And I think every footballer needs a bit of help and encouragement from time to time."

Shilton would have the edge over Clemence in any poll on the issue among England's League managers, coaches and footballers. In November 1978, at a time when Ron Greenwood was keeping faith with Clemence as England's first choice, the London Evening News conducted a survey among First Division attacking midfield men and forwards on the question of who was the better of the two 'keepers. Of the 22 players asked to give their views, nine voted for Shilton and only two for Clemence, one of them being Clemence's Liverpool teammate David Johnson. Eleven could not decide. This is what some of them said:

Joe Mercer (left with Shilton) and Don Revie (right), the England managers who made Clemence the No. 1 goalkeeper in their squads, at Shilton's expense.

Shilton played in only the first four of England's seven matches under the caretaker-managership of Mercer, and in no more than three of the 31 matches when Revie was in charge. A bitter pill to swallow for a man who had previously established himself as the ideal successor to Gordon Banks at international level, and who seemed set to remain England's first choice 'keeper for a number of years.

Of Revie, Shilton recalls: "I just couldn't understand it, and in the end I got so sick of him not even giving me a confidence-booster that I just said: 'Right, that's it'."

Shilton told Revie he no longer wished to be considered for the England squad and, although he was subsequently persuaded to change his mind, his resentment towards Revie remained: "On the day I first met him, I had a feeling that he and I weren't going to get on."

Andy Gray: "I have always rated Shilton above Clemence. In my opinion, he has the edge in most goalkeeping departments."

Liam Brady: "Clemence is very quick off his line, Shilton is very agile for a big man. I can't say who is better."

David Johnson: "England are very lucky to have the two best goalkeepers in the world. But I think Clemence is the best in the business. He is a born goalkeeper, a man who is built like a goalkeeper. By comparison, Shilton seems manufactured. At the moment he is in brilliant form but he hasn't got Clemence's natural ability."

Whatever the varying opinions, many of Shilton's fellow professionals argue that he's even better than Gordon Banks, even though Banks collected 73 caps, an all-time England record for a goalkeeper. George Dewis, who helped train both men at Leicester, feels that Shilton is "more powerful in the air" than Banks was "and more agile possibly." Matt Gillies, the former Leicester manager, also suggests that Shilton is better, while ex-Stoke boss Tony Waddington, makes them "all-square".

Says Waddington: "Well, they're totally different types you see ... Peter is more of a strength goalkeeper – he's had to adjust his technique to his build and has got the absolute maximum out of it. He is tremendously strong in all his saves, whereas Gordon, I think, perhaps got to the ball a bit earlier because of his litheness and mobility."

It's difficult to imagine, however, any goal-keeper – even Clemence and Banks – inspiring a more fanatical hero-worship in another man filling the same position than Shilton has in 30-year-old John Burridge, of Queen's Park Rangers. Burridge was setting out on his career at Workington when Shilton was in the Leicester first team at 17 or 18 and he has since modelled himself on him. "People say it's wrong to copy, but I think it's flippin' good to copy, especially if you're following someone like Peter Shilton," says Burridge, who feels that he's always possessed the same inborn drive and determination.

Burridge once took a photograph of Shilton to his barber so that he could give him the same hairstyle. He was at Blackpool when Shilton was at Stoke and it was then that the two first met. "The wife and I were travelling through Stoke one Sunday," Burridge recalls, "and I just went to Stoke centre-forward John Ritchie's house and got him to ring Shilts to ask if I could come over to see him." Shilton and Burridge spent all afternoon together and have kept in touch ever since.

Shilton is now practically a confidant and counsellor to Burridge. His influence on him is particularly evident when Burridge recounts his experiences at his next two clubs, Aston Villa and Crystal Palace. Villa bought him for £100,000 in September 1975 but his three years there were far from happy because, Burridge claims, the manager Ron Saunders, wouldn't allow him to dictate how his defence should play. When Palace then bought Burridge for £50,000, in March 1978, he played a big part in helping to steer a basically very young and inexperienced team to the Second Division Championship in 1978/79 and, for a brief period the following season, to the top of the First Division. But Burridge fell out with Palace because they wouldn't pay him what he felt he was worth.

"I wouldn't say boo to a goose when I was in my mid-twenties," Burridge says. "I thought I was getting good pay at Villa until I heard what others were getting. At Palace I wanted to be the top man because I was the top man on the field. I *knew* what I was worth ... I knew what I'd done for them and I thought that if they lost me they'd go down. I told the manager that. I said: 'Look, you'll get better goalkeepers than me, better shot-stoppers or cross-takers, but you'll not get someone who can influence players, make them play like I do'."

In his own fashion Burridge echoes much of what Shilton privately feels about the differences between Clemence and himself. Burridge, for example, insists that Shilton has had more outstanding games for England than Clemence. He also argues a point which will not be lost on the non-prejudiced by suggesting that Clemence might have been "flattered" as a result of being in such good teams. It is true that Liverpool have long been renowned for their ability in defence, and while this has provided a stern test of Clemence's concentration (nothing is more difficult for a goalkeeper than suddenly being forced into action after a long period in which he's had little to do), Burridge proposes the not unreasonable idea that Clemence's overall technical attributes and temperament were never really fully tested there.

"Peter Shilton has been the mainstay of his teams, everybody knows that," Burridge says. "Nottingham Forest won the European Cup two seasons in succession, but if you'd taken Peter out of that team, what would you have got? Just a normal side. No disrespect to Ray Clemence, but what would have happened if you had put him in some of the teams Shilts has played for at Leicester, Stoke and Nottingham Forest? It's been much easier for him

at Liverpool – my mother could play in goal for Liverpool sometimes."

To Shilton, Clemence's advantage in this respect was particularly pronounced during the time he (Shilton) was at Stoke City, from November 1974 to September 1977. Shilton feels it significant that Stoke's decline coincided with Clemence gaining a regular place in the England team. Stoke had paid Leicester a princely sum for him and his "invincible" reputation. It was to cost him dearly for Shilton inevitably found himself under closer scrutiny than anyone during Stoke's slide into the Second Division. He insists, somewhat resentfully, that his form was made to look a lot worse than it really was by the failings of the men in front of him.

Sir Alf Ramsey was England's manager when Shilton was first brought into the England squad, and it was under Ramsey that he experienced his

Shilton, down but never out. He is sensitive to any suggestion that he isn't the No. 1 goalkeeper in Britain, or indeed the world, so much so that such a view is always liable to bring the best out of him. "I don't like being looked upon as the same as someone else and, if necessary, I'll be striving to prove myself better than anyone else to the end of my days."

happiest spell in international football. Although Shilton was left out of the squad for the 1970 World Cup Finals in Mexico, he made his debut in a 3-1 win over East Germany at Wembley in November of that year (England's first match after the World Cup). By the time Ramsey was sacked in 1974, Shilton had made a total of 16 appearances in 30 matches, and begun to establish himself as England's first-choice 'keeper in succession to Gordon Banks. Then came Shilton's turning point . . . he played in only the first four of England's seven matches under the caretaker-managership of Joe Mercer and three of their 31 matches under Don Revie.

In May 1976 Shilton was so tormented by the situation that just before England were due to depart on a three-match tour of the United States he told Revie that he no longer wished to be considered for England selection. At that time, Shilton had made no more than one appearance in England's 16 games following Revie's appointment as manager (the 5-0 win against Cyprus at Wembley in April 1975) and he recalls:

"I was upset, not so much because Revie chose to make me his No. 2 goalkeeper, but that he didn't give me the chance to show what I could do. It was tremendous to get that game against Cyprus, don't misunderstand me, but it wasn't the best game in which a goalkeeper could prove himself. What really got me about the situation was that Revie kept coming up to me and saying: 'The difference between you and Ray is just paper thin.' But every time the team sheet went up I was never on it. Never got a game, even against teams like Wales and Northern Ireland. I just couldn't understand it and in the end, I got so sick of him not even giving me a confidence-booster, that I just said: 'Right, that's it'."

Other managers might have turned their backs on Shilton, but during the tour of the States, which West Ham's 'keeper Phil Parkes (then with Queen's Park Rangers) also decided to miss because of personal reasons, the performances of Revie's replacement 'keepers, Jimmy Rimmer and Joe Corrigan, prompted him to try and persuade Shilton to come back into the squad.

Revie says that Rimmer and Corrigan had been magnificent on the occasions he'd watched them at club level, but that when it came to taking over from Clemence and Shilton in the England team "they didn't seem to have much confidence in themselves." Rimmer was selected for England's second match on that tour – the 3-2 win over Italy – with Corrigan named as one of the substitutes and Revie recalls that when the team were due to leave for the stadium, Rimmer, "looking extremely nervous" asked if he could travel without his jacket and tie. "When I travel to a match with a jacket and tie on I never do well," he explained. "Let's compromise," Revie replied, having previously stipulated that all players must wear suits and ties when going to and from matches. "Take them off when you are on the coach, and put them back on when we got to the ground." Revie felt that Rimmer looked ill at ease

in the opening 20 minutes of the game, when Italy established a 2-0 lead and Corrigan, whom he brought on for the second half, "wasn't as confident as I expected either."

Revie contacted Shilton almost immediately he returned to England and Shilton says: "He invited me to come back and I think I asked him whether I'd get more games. Fair enough, he did say: 'No, I can't promise that.' But I made my point as far as I could see and was prepared to accept the situation. I did get one or two games for England after that, but why I couldn't have had them in the first place, I don't know."

Shilton's two other England appearances under Revie came in the 1977 British International Championship, in a 2-1 win against Northern Ireland in Belfast and, three days later, a 1-0 defeat by Wales at Wembley. The first match stands out in Shilton's mind because in the last few minutes he denied the Irish what seemed a certain equaliser and, as he was walking off the field at the end, Revie put an arm around his shoulders and told him that he'd "saved the game" for England.

A seemingly laudable gesture, but Shilton's resentment for Revie led him to interpret it in a rather different way.

"He was all over me," Shilton says. "Being the way I am, it rubbed me up the wrong way I'm afraid. I couldn't understand him making such a fuss about me after selecting me only twice in three years." What would Shilton have done in Revie's shoes? "Well, the last thing I would have done would have been to walk on the pitch like that, because of one important save. I'd have come into the dressing room and maybe said something like: 'Well, I played Peter Shilton today to give him a game and he did exceptionally well.' That would have been it for me."

Shilton admits that he failed to take to Revie right from the beginning. "You get a feeling about people," Shilton says, "and on the day I first met him, I got the feeling that he and I weren't going to get on."

He disagreed with a number of Revie's methods, was particularly critical of Revie for making so many team changes (thus failing to establish a settled side), and didn't like the way Revie gave vent to his emotions publicly in times of crisis. He recalls being irritated by the sight of Revie in tears after England's 2-0 defeat by Italy in the crucial World Cup qualifying tie in November 1976.

"I didn't think it was right . . . I certainly didn't think it was right to cry in front of the press, that's for sure. Bobby Charlton could be seen shedding tears from time to time, but Charlton was that type of man. That's one of the reasons why I think he didn't make it as a manager – he wasn't strong enough.

"But when you get someone like Don Revie, who has proved he can be a right tough, competitive so-an-so, well, it just disturbed me."

Shilton is also critical of Joe Mercer, the other England manager to decide that Clemence had the slight edge on him. Shilton felt he did reasonably well in England's first four matches under Mercer, against Wales (2–0), Ireland (1–0), Scotland (0–2) and Argentina (2–2). Consequently he expected to keep his place in the team for their subsequent three-match tour of Eastern Europe.

"Joe Mercer came up to me before the first match (against East Germany) and said: 'No detriment to the way you've been playing, but I'd like to give Ray Clemence and one or two other members of the squad a game.' I was under the impression that it was only going to be temporary and thought: 'Fair enough'. But Ray, who had a good game, stayed in the team for the other two matches against Bulgaria and Yugoslavia and then Don Revie took over . . .

"There must have been a reason why Joe Mercer preferred Ray Clemence to me and it annoyed me that he didn't tell me. I thought he should have been big enough to come up to me and explain the situation."

Shilton inevitably talks in much more glowing terms about Sir Alf Ramsey, a man not unlike Shilton in that he, too, had a reputation for stubbornness during his football career and gave outsiders the impression of being a rather cold, remote figure. "I used to think the world of Sir Alf," Shilton says, "because he gave me my chance in international football and stuck by me. Not only this, he was my type of man, a strong man who left no-one in any doubt that he was the boss."

Despite Ramsey's aloofness even with his England teams Shilton, at 19, got a rare glimpse of the other side of the national team manager after his debut for the England Under-23 team against Wales at Birmingham in 1969. There was a post-game reception for the teams and officials and Shilton recalls: "I was in awe of the man. It was my first England match and I was finding it hard to relax with him sitting at the top of our table. But then the drinks started flowing and after two or three gin-and-tonics, Alf started loosening up a bit. An elderly FA official came across, shook Alf's hand and wished

everybody all the best and Alf just muttered 'Silly sod' as he walked away. I thought: 'Bloody hell, the man's human!'"

Shilton learned to admire Ramsey for the atmosphere he created in the England squads. "The squad was like a family, and once you got in there, he'd stand by you through thick and thin," he says. "All the men in that squad were made to feel important, and that playing for England was important." And Shilton learned also to respect Ramsey for his knowledge of the game and his pre-match tactical briefings. "There was one stage in my career when I took my dominating style to the extreme. I began to get into the habit of coming too far off my line for shots from the edge of the penalty area and was positioning myself well outside the six-yard box. Alf noticed this and during training one day he just came up to me and said: 'Don't you think you may be a little too far off your line?' I told him I didn't think so and that was the end of it. But I thought about it afterwards and realised he was right.

"One of the great things about him," Shilton adds, "is that Alf didn't complicate the game. He made good basic points but never got too involved.

"People have often asked me how such an apparently cold man could motivate teams, but he could you know. He saved what I would call the emotional team talks for the most important matches. Take the World Cup qualifying tie against Poland . . . I've never heard a talk quite like the one he gave that night. Brian Clough and Peter Taylor have given some really inspiring ones at Nottingham Forest but Ramsey did it on his own. I can't remember exactly what he said, but the tone of it was such that by the time he'd finished we all felt we had to beat the Poles for the whole of England."

Over the years Shilton has played for England at every level. He was a member of the England Youth team which reached the Final of the "Little World Cup" (and lost to Russia 1–0) in Turkey in 1967. Since then it has always been his burning ambition to set the seal on an already remarkable career by appearing in the final stages of a senior World Cup.

When England were beaten by Poland in the qualifying competiton for the 1974 World Cup, a senior player told Shilton: "Do you realise that of all the players available to the England team at the moment, you are the one in the strongest position to get 100 or more caps, like Bobby Moore and Bobby Charlton?"

Shilton prefers to forget the observation. The memory of it can easily drive him into a very black mood.

Sir Alf Ramsey (right) and Ron Greenwood (above), the England managers who have provided the bright spots in Shilton's international career. It was under Ramsey, England's manager when the national side won the World Cup in 1966, that Shilton made his debut in the team, against East Germany at Wembley in November 1970. Ramsey then installed him as England's first-choice 'keeper in succession to Gordon Banks.

"I used to think the world of Sir Alf," Shilton recalls. "He was my type of man . . . a strong man who left no-one in any doubt that he was the boss."

Shilton also admired Ramsey because "he didn't complicate the game. He made good basic points but never got too involved."

Greenwood, mindful of the blow to Shilton's pride through being forced to accept second-billing to Clemence under Don Revie and Joe Mercer, decided to play the two goalkeepers in alternate matches, on a sort of rota basis.

Shilton has mixed feelings about the policy ("No two players can be exactly the same . . . one must be better than the other.") but, nevertheless, he speaks highly of Greenwood: "A nice man, with a tremendous knowledge of international football and a lot of original ideas. I've got on well with him."

8

THE PRESSURE POT

Peter and Sue Shilton, with their two sons, Michael, 8 (left) and Sam, 3 (right).

Peter Shilton has read only one book from cover to cover in the last five years: Jimmy Greaves's highly-acclaimed autobiography "This One's on Me".

The opening paragraph of Greaves's book reads: "My name is Jimmy Greaves. I am a professional footballer and I am an alcoholic." Greaves, the idol of millions during his days as an outstanding goal-scorer, goes on to explain how he collapsed under the pressures at the top, began a slow descent into alcoholism which wrecked his career and marriage ...and how, with the help of Alcoholics Anonymous, he fought back and regained his self-respect.

"To an outsider, it must have looked as if I had everything going for me," Greaves writes. "International footballer, successful businessman, happily married with four great kids, a marvellous house surrounded by admiring friends. But if you delve deeply into the life and times of Jimmy Greaves, you'll find the answers to why I turned to the bottle for comfort and escape."

It started, Greaves explains, when his four-month-old son died of pneumonia and he was involved in a traumatic transfer from Chelsea to the Italian club AC Milan. "I needed drink to help blot out the nightmare I was living," he says.

Then, when he moved to Tottenham four months later: "I drank heavily to relieve the pressure of big-time football and by the time I joined West Ham, I was into the early stages of alcoholism where I drank because I *needed* to."

The book made a considerable impact on Shilton – and his wife Sue – because he himself had begun to feel the strain of being at the top.

Shilton's crisis point came during the 1980/81 season. It was a bad one for Nottingham Forest, with the team repeatedly being changed to accommodate new signings and failing to win any competition. And for Shilton, too, it was a particularly unhappy season. In addition to his disappointment at Forest's decline, the cumulative effect of the high number of matches he'd played over a period of 15 years caught up with him. It was to eventually prompt him to drop out of the England squad for their run of six matches at the season's end in favour of taking a complete break from the game. But there were also problems outside football.

Shilton attracted a mammoth amount of adverse publicity – and abuse from crowds – following a drunken night out. He was discovered with a married woman in his red Daimler car in the early hours (by an irate husband), and after hitting a lamp-post with his car was breathalysed by the police and banned from driving for 15 months.

The tension in the Shilton household, as a result, was inevitable and then further aggravated by an intensification of rumours in Nottingham concerning the Shiltons' marriage. Peter and Sue's relationship had been going through a bad patch even before the "Tina Street Saga" and the digging into their private life by newspaper reporters served to make worse an already delicate situation.

It is against this troubled background that Shilton's habit of having an occasional night out by himself following a spell of high-pressure matches – to get the tension out of his system – must be viewed. He began to take these "blow-outs", as he calls them, to the extreme.

At one stage Sue Shilton, distressed by her husband's low spirits and the failure of herself and some of their friends to lift him out of them, tried to enlist the help of Brian Clough. She met Clough in his office at the City Ground, without Shilton's knowledge, but didn't find the Forest manager as sympathetic as she had expected. Clough intimated that Shilton and herself should sort out such problems themselves and, feeling that she might have over-reacted, she telephoned Clough the following day to apologise for having troubled him with the matter.

Peter and Sue Shilton did eventually leap the traumatic hurdle in their lives ... but not before a particularly bad spell in which Shilton seemed to be sinking deeper into his depression, relying increasingly on his favourite drink, champagne, to help blot out the torment.

A great horse-racing fan, the turning point for him came towards the end of the season when he went to Cheltenham to watch the Gold Cup on Thursday March 19, the day after Forest's 1–1 draw at Manchester United. His depression, combined with too much champagne and symptoms of 'flu, prompted him to spend the night in a Cheltenham hotel. His intention was to get a hire car back to Nottingham at 7am for the following day's training. The next morning, however, Shilton felt so unwell that he missed training and didn't travel back until after lunch. By the time he arrived back in Nottingham, at 5pm, influenza had taken a real grip on him and he could hardly walk or talk.

Sue Shilton had never seen him in such a state of helplessness and her immediate response was to call the family doctor to him. Their GP too was quick to note the seriousness of the situation and after giving Shilton a thorough examination, he prescribed a course of penicillin for his influenza and left him with the warning: "If you don't forget about football and stay in bed for at least two weeks, you're going to be in serious trouble."

Shilton missed the match at West Bromwich Albion that Saturday and also the England–Spain friendly at Wembley three days later, but was back in Forest's team for the home match against Norwich City the following Saturday.

The shock of being on the brink of a slight breakdown got him through the remainder of the season, in which he played well, too. Then he spent much of the summer with Sue and their two children, Michael 8 and Sam 3, at the cottage he'd bought in the tiny Devon village of Bigbury, 15 miles from Plymouth. It helped to restore him to "normality".

As he says now, when talking about the pressures of the game: "I understand so well what Jimmy Greaves was getting at in his book, it isn't true."

It can be argued that the pressures Shilton feels are self-created by the intensity and single-mindedness of his approach to the game. Many men who have worked with Shilton feel that he takes himself and the game too seriously. "The biggest difference between Peter and I," says Mark Wallington, "is that I bring more humour to the game. Whether that's a good thing or a bad thing, I don't know – it's for other people to judge – but, for me, it's difficult to see how anyone can get any enjoyment out of it if they're too intense.

"You know, I've never seen Peter laugh on a football field. Don't misunderstand me, I can understand why he's so serious, but I've got to have some release valve, a laugh and a joke. Whatever our result on a Saturday, I'll always pop into our local for a couple of pints at Sunday lunch-time. In Peter's case, it's not his style."

Although Shilton's ultra-dedicated approach to the game has invariably caused him to become something of an isolated figure, even among his own teammates, this is something which he has encouraged. It has helped to ensure that the dominating role he fills in his teams, the influence he has on the men around him, is not weakened by them getting too close to him. Not only this, Shilton wants to be, and seen to be, different to other footballers. He doesn't think this can be achieved through repeatedly mixing with them socially.

"I isolate myself because I want to be my own man," he says. "People can see too much of you, get to know you too much – it's just not me. In any case, I can't get close because I'm too involved with myself."

There are times when Shilton feels the need to isolate himself from his family also. Thus despite the sordid front page newspaper headlines, following the night he landed in trouble with the police and the husband of the woman he was with, he has continued to spend the odd evening out at a local wine bar or nightclub – without Sue.

"She doesn't think that married men should go out on their own, and if I were in her position I suppose I'd feel the same way," Shilton says. "But she accepts it because she appreciates that I need to relax in this way to do my job properly and, despite that incident a while ago, she trusts me not to abuse this sort of freedom.

"It's funny when you talk about me being too intense in my approach to football, because this is precisely one of the ways I've tried to avoid that. About five years ago I decided that I wasn't going to live a life totally dictated by football, working at the game non-stop and living like a monk.

"If I'd tried to do that, there's no way I'd have produced such a consistently high standard of performance. It's impossible to be at 100 per cent throughout an entire season. But you can get close to it, and the way you do that is to know when and how to work, and when and how to enjoy yourself. It's a question of finding the right balance.

"I realised that, by dedicating myself to football, I could easily end up at 35 or 40 having never had any fun."

"The trouble is, I'm like my mum, in that I've got loads of nervous energy and when I make my mind up to do something, then I do it – no holds barred. My mind's on football so much, even when I'm sitting at home. You know, people think a footballer's day is ended when he's finished his two hours training, but it isn't so with me. I get so worked up about it that some days, I've just got to get out, do something else, to take my mind off it."

"So if I want to go out on my own for a drink, I won't think: 'Oh, you shouldn't do that', I'll just do it and people can think what they want."

Helpful to Shilton is his particular interest in dog and horse racing.

During the early part of his career at Leicester City, Shilton bought some greyhounds and trained them himself. Eventually, he gave them to his City coach, George Dewis, when his interest in the sport faded. He has since become much more interested in horse racing, which he follows most days with the help of the newspaper, The Sporting Life, and TV. He bought his first horse, Admiral Jersey, for £1,500. He is proud of the fact that it finished fifth at Wolverhampton as a two-year-old and, when it

Left, Peter and Sue Shilton on their wedding day, September 27, 1970. "A great day," Shilton recalls, with a smile. "A lovely reception and everything went perfectly." Shilton, typical of a man who pays meticulous attention to detail, ensured that the day would be remembered by arranging for the wedding ceremony to be tape-recorded, and a cine film to be taken of the reception.

Above, the Shiltons today, outside their four-bedroom, detached house in the "desirable" Nottingham suburb of West Bridgford. It had five bedrooms when Shilton bought it for £31,000 in 1977, but one was sacrificed so that he could have an outsize bathroom incorporating a sauna and solarium.

The Shiltons have spent more than £10,000 on improving the property and among its other striking features is a well-furnished and decorated sun lounge. Shilton ("I was quite good at art at school.") designed the interior of the house himself.

One of two Shilton properties, the other is a cottage in the Devon village of Bigbury, 15 miles from Plymouth: "It's our retreat," Shilton says. "A place where we can unwind and be ourselves."

didn't train on, he got back what he paid for it. He then bought Dark Hope and a half-share in Twice a Star but they were both sold at a slight loss because of illness. His latest horse is Prickles, a five-year old acquired at the Newmarket sales two years ago and trained by Basil Richmond near Newark.

"It's not raced very much because we've had to have it gelded," Shilton says.

Not surprisingly, the fact that Shilton likes to gamble on the horses, and the roulette wheel in Nottingham's Victoria Gaming Club, has not gone unnoticed by the rumourmongers.

One one occasion, the owner of the Victoria Club telephoned Shilton to tell him that two newspaper reporters in his office were claiming to have received a letter stating that Shilton owed the club £35,000 in gambling losses.

"Would you like to say anything to them before I throw them out?" the owner asked him. Shilton, flabbergasted, turned down the invitation.

On another occasion one newspaper with visions of a confession-of-a-compulsive-gambler type of story, like that of Orient's Stan Bowles, made an offer to Shilton through his agent Jon Holmes. They wanted an exclusive interview on what is a non-existent subject as far as Shilton is concerned. "You must be joking," said Holmes, before curtailing the conversation abruptly.

Shilton is, in fact, reluctant to discuss his gambling in depth. He is not embarrassed by it, but feels it's a personal matter, "something people shouldn't talk about in the sense of 'I've won this', or 'I've lost that'." He admits that he might sometimes stake what many people would consider "huge" amounts of money. But, as he points out, they are not particularly big sums if taken in relation to what he earns:

"You can't win when you talk about gambling because it's generally looked upon as a weakness," Shilton says. "You know, I don't like losing at anything but even if I've done a few hundred quid on a day at the races, I still come back relaxed and feel that I've had a good day. I was talking about it to a friend of mine the other day, a businessman, and I was telling him how much it relaxes me. I said to him: 'Don't you ever fancy a bet?' and he replied: 'Well, to be quite truthful I gamble every day. I'm gambling all the time, because I've got stocks and shares and some days I'll pick up a paper and see I'm losing £1,000 on them and other days I'll see that I've got it all back again.'

"Same difference isn't it? Buying an old car is a gamble – in fact, life's a gamble. I'm not saying I've been an angel and only bet £5 here and there, but I won't talk about the amounts of money I've wagered. To me the important thing is the overall picture."

So where did the rumours about him being £35,000 in debt to the Victoria Club spring from? He shakes his head and frowns. "Don't ask me." He then smiles and adds: "Tell me, do I look as if I'm in debt?"

A good point. Shilton earns around £90,000 a year from football, not including the £15,000-plus he gets from such items as advertising and endorsements. The main sources of this extra income are: Puma (boots) £4,000; Sandico (gloves, balls) £1,500; Coffer (jerseys) £5,000; IPC Magazines, Exclusive Press Features Ltd (newspaper and magazine columns) £5,000. "It could be a lot more," Jon Holmes says, "but it's more important to us that Peter gets involved in the right things image-wise."

Shilton, who will start drawing a considerable pension from the age of 35, is not short of capital assets either, with two cars (Sue has a mini) and, of course, two houses. His house in Nottingham is an imposing, four-bedroom detached property (valued at £90,000) in West Bridgford, a "desirable" suburb just a mile or two from the Forest ground at Trent Bridge. It had five bedrooms when Shilton bought it in 1977 for £31,500, but one was sacrificed so that he could have an outsize bathroom incorporating a sauna and solarium. Another particularly striking feature, the result of the £10,000-plus he initially spent on improving the property, is an exquisitely decorated and furnished sun lounge. The inside of the house, tastefully furnished and decorated, was designed by Shilton himself. The attention to detail he brought to the task is reflected in his irritation at a small mark on the leg of a reproduction antique chair, caused by Sam Shilton gnawing at it when he was cutting his teeth.

Shilton is the first to admit that he is not the easiest of people to live with. "I can be selfish," he says. "But when you are as single-minded as I am in my football career, it's difficult to be entirely different away from it. I look at other top professional sportsmen and I see the same faults in them that I've got in me. Geoff Boycott, for example: he's not married, and looking at the way he's dedicated himself to cricket, I'm not surprised.

"Some people would argue that I shouldn't have got married because you have to be so dedicated, and get so screwed up with your profession, that it's unfair on the other person. You know, I watched John McEnroe at Wimbledon on TV – I could see his frustration building up and I could understand it totally. He's like me, a little bit highly strung, but I'm older and have learned to temper it."

Almost everything in the Shilton household revolves around his needs and requirements. Sue Shilton says: "You have to know him exactly to be right in tune with him. You have to know when he doesn't want you, when he wants the children and doesn't want them . . ."

But she isn't complaining. On the wall of their breakfast room is a small Virgo plaque (Shilton's astrological sign) which she bought for him. It reads: "I'm a perfectionist, but that's because I pay so much attention to detail. In life I might appear cold but I'm really sincere and always willing to give."

She also bought him a metal key-ring, on which was engraved this message:

When you're sad, I cry,
And when you hurt I bleed,
I feel your pain,
And I know your thoughts,
So when all else crumbles to the ground,
I will stand as your support . . .

To a number of women, Sue Shilton would appear to have built her life around her husband to the extent of sacrificing much of her own individuality as a person. She does not look upon it that way.

"His mum helped make him the way he is and I've carried on from her," she says. "Some days, he'll go into a shell at home and shut himself off from everything and everybody. I allow him to do that. If he's sitting there and I can sense that he doesn't want to be bothered by anybody, I'll just shut the door and leave him to it . . ."

"For example, there are times when I've sat and watched the TV in the morning room all night, while he's been watching the TV in the lounge.

"I understand why he needs to shut himself off and generally I agree with it because I think I have a good life. It's part of his job and that job has given us a nice house and a lot of luxury things which a lot of other people can't have.

"At one time, I used to think that I wasn't really contributing anything to him in his career, but now I know differently. Cooking and looking after children might not seem very important, but as a so-called celebrity, Peter needs someone normal to come home to and bring him back to earth."

Her importance to Shilton goes deeper than that, of course. Shilton won a Sports Personality of the Year Award in 1979 and the following year the organisers telephoned to ask for the trophy to be returned so that they could hand it to the 1980 winner, Sebastian Coe.

"We're just lending it to you because we'll have it back next year," Sue said, in front of Shilton. She then turned to him and told him: "In the meantime I want something to put in its place."

"Basically," says Shilton, "I like to think I can do all the motivating myself. But sometimes, Sue will say something . . . it's amazing the way she does it."

Sue, an attractive, 31-year-old blonde, met Shilton at a Leicester nightclub when she was 17 and working as a secretary in a solicitor's office. They were engaged two years later and married in 1970, when she was 20. Both her sons have the same colouring as her.

She says she is more romantic than her husband. "He has his moments," she says. "But he's romantic in his way, not mine. I'm a bit silly and sloppy with it. You know, if we're out together I'd love us to hold hands, but no way would he do anything like that if he thinks people are looking at him." However, he does pay her plenty of compliments and has been known to surprise her with *his* romantic way. Like the time when she decided to take a short break from him with the children, at their cottage in Bigbury. The day she arrived, she received a large bunch of flowers from him. "I rang up and asked him if his mother had sent them," she recalls, mischievously.

In a lot of ways they are very much alike – too much so she feels. She can be every bit as stubborn and aggressive as he is, and she admits this makes for a relationship which can be potentially explosive.

Shilton, smiling broadly, emphasises the point with a story concerning the mini car he bought her for a surprise Christmas present in 1977. He arranged for a friend to drive it to the Shilton home late on Christmas Eve, and leave it outside the garage, with a large ribbon around it. "On Christmas eve," Shilton recalls, "she was trying to get me to give her a clue about what I'd bought for her, and I said that I hadn't even had time to get her a card. With that, she tore up the card she'd got me, threw it in the dustbin and went to bed with the hump."

The following morning, Shilton got her to go outside the house on the pretence that their dog had run into the street. Upon seeing the car, she returned with tears streaming down her face.

"I had to go in for training that morning," he adds, "but by the time I got back she'd taken her card to me out of the bin, somehow put it together again, and it was propped up on the mantelpiece like a bit of wet lettuce."

"If anything upsets me, I can't keep it hidden," she says. "I have to say what I think – there's no diplomacy in me at all. Occasionally I think that he could really do with someone who's very calm and quiet."

It's that stubbornness and fighting spirit, however, which has helped the Shiltons overcome any problems in their marriage, and in particular the pressure that descended upon them after what they both refer to as Shilton's "accident". Her initial mood of anger and resentment, her feeling of having been "cheated", gradually gave way to one of defiance.

Facing page, Shilton with the family's pet labrador, Julie. Above and left, showing Michael and Sam a trick or two – or is it the other way around? Sam, the three-year-old, has been nicknamed "Road Runner" because "all day long he's running around at 100 miles an hour."

Meanwhile, eight-year-old Michael is now developing a wide range of sporting interests, but he particularly enjoys soccer – and swimming. "Sue's an excellent swimmer and Michael takes after her," says Shilton.

"Those people, expecting our marriage to crumble as a result of all this, are going to be disappointed," she said at the time. "There's no way I am going to allow all that we have built up over the last 10 years to be destroyed without putting up a fight."

Nowadays, Sue will even occasionally rib him about the "accident". The only bitterness remaining is directed towards the media and those who used it as ammunition to "give him stick".

"I felt more sorry for Peter than I did for myself," she says. "He's done too much for football to have been treated the way he was because of one isolated mistake or whatever you want to call it."

Shilton, too, was bitter about the attitude of some "so-called" football fans towards him. "They pay their money, and I suppose they are entitled to shout what they want," he says, "but I was still disappointed that they made me a target. These sort of people aren't interested in watching football matches – all they're interested in is having a go at someone, and if they hadn't been having a go at me, they'd have been chanting insults at the referee or their own players.

"But it didn't worry me on the field – indeed, I found it a bit of a spur."

One of the matches in which Shilton was taunted by fans was Nottingham Forest's friendly at Grantham in December 1980. The game was arranged to give the non-League club a financial boost, after its expenditure on new floodlights.

"We were doing them a favour," Shilton points out and I was absolutely disgusted at what some of the spectators behind my goal were shouting at me." At half-time, Shilton, incensed, told Peter Taylor that he wasn't "going to bother going out for the second half," but Taylor managed to appease him.

One of the biggest problems of being as successful and famous as Shilton is that one can rarely get away from the public eye. Unfortunately, unlike a lot of superstars, Shilton has never come to terms with living his life in a goldfish bowl. Shilton insists that it's been particularly tiresome in his own case because he was born and bred in the Midlands, and spent all his career playing for clubs in small towns or cities there.

The frustration of not being able to go anywhere in that part of the world, without being instantly recognised and approached for his autograph or a chat about football, has led to him becoming almost a recluse in his family life.

He enjoys, for instance, taking Sue and the children into the country on a Sunday, but such days out are often spoilt for him to a certain extent when people, unwittingly, will not allow him to sink into the background.

Not long ago, the Shiltons went to a Leicestershire hotel for lunch. He went to the bar to order some drinks and immediately found himself the centre of attraction.

The woman serving behind the bar looked at him, incredulously.

"It's not, is it?"

"What do you mean, love," Shilton replied.

"It's not who I think it is ... it's not Peter Shilton?"

"Yes love, afraid it is."

"Oh," she cried out. "We've got PETER SHILTON here."

Many famous personalities enjoy such recognition but not Shilton. There are times when he can become almost neurotic about it.

"I've started to get a bit offish with people," he admits. "Some people seem to regard you as their property and it really does get on your nerves. You can be talking to somebody and they'll suddenly recognise you and come up and start talking to you, right in the middle of a conversation you're having. Some of them are so rude. They'll approach you for your autograph, but instead of saying, 'Oh, excuse me, have you got time to sign this for me please', they'll just thrust the book at you and say: 'Oh, come on, sign this for us!'

"People also tend to be caught by surprise when they recognise you, and say something totally stupid." Shilton recalls one night when he and a friend (Gravesend FC chairman Roger Easterby) went to a restaurant at Lingfield, Surrey, with their wives. While they were having aperitifs at the bar, a man walked in with his family, pointed at Shilton and exclaimed: 'Oh look, it's Shilton." Shilton's embarrassment can still be seen when he talks about that incident today.

"I suppose we have a reasonable social life," he adds, "but there aren't many places in Nottingham where you can feel totally relaxed. If I go out for the evening alone, I'll never go to a pub – I don't like to be seen standing at a bar because it's not me. Pubs are for social talk and you know what people are like; they get a few drinks inside them and they want to start exchanging views on the game with you. Therefore I prefer to go to a nightclub for a meal and a drink because, with people listening to the music or eyeing up the birds, you tend to be lost in the crowd a bit more."

He looks hurt when you suggest he's anti-social.

"Look, I don't mind signing autographs and chatting to people – most times I enjoy it – but sometimes you want some privacy to just enjoy yourself with your family."

Shilton is particularly sensitive about the effect of his fame on his family. That's why he rarely takes Sue out shopping and rarely takes his family out to public places. "Sue takes them to fairs and things like that," he says.

"There'd be no point me doing so because I wouldn't be able to relax and you know they wouldn't be able to relax either. Kids are following me, chanting my name, that sort of thing and how can any day out like that be enjoyable?"

Sue Shilton is inclined to agree. "I don't like going out shopping with him," she says. "Because when I'm on my own I'm nobody, whereas when I'm with him I'm Mrs. Shilton. Being well known doesn't interest me at all. You know, when we go into a restaurant, the owner or the waiter will say: 'Hello Mrs. Shilton, how are you?' and really he'll only be talking to me like that because I'm with Peter. I bet that if I were to walk into the same restaurant by myself, I wouldn't be recognised. It's something I have to live with but I don't like it."

Shilton attempts to shield his two sons from this sort of pressure; he has never visited the private school Michael attends on one of its open days or sports days. "I take an interest in what he does at school," Shilton says, "but I think it would be bad for him if I went there. The other lads would be whispering, 'Oh, there's Peter Shilton', and making a big thing out of it and it might unsettle him. "I will go there when he's a bit older, but for the time being I feel it's important that I allow him to be himself."

Shilton's superstar status is also reflected by the number of letters he receives. He gets an average of 100 letters a month, many from parts of the world outside of Britain, including Taiwan and Botswana. With the assistance of the secretary of his friend and business adviser Jon Holmes, he replies to all but the handful which are abusive or obscene. Letters come from charity organisations requesting goalkeeping kit for auctions or raffles, from young supporters asking for autographed photographs and from others seeking advice on ways to improve their own playing ability. A cross-section:

"May I please have your old Forest goalkeeping shirt? I have been a fan of yours for four years. I am now seven. I have got money saved to buy it. I think you are the best goalkeeper in all the world."

David, Lincolnshire.

"Please can you tell me how and where you started goalkeeping and how you found a professional club? Do you have any pre-match rituals? What boots do you use? What is it like to play in the final of a European Cup and FA Cup? What training do you do for goalkeeping? Can you tell me how to prepare for trials with clubs? What gloves do you use and what do you do with your old gloves? Please can I buy a pair of your old gloves off you so I can put them in a specially-made frame and display them in my bedroom? Do you have any old things, such as studs from your boots or laces, so I can put these in a frame and display them, too?"

Paul, 16, Glossop.

"I am currently in goal for Selston Crown Inn, playing in the Alfreton and Sunday League Division III. I am 19 and 5 ft 6 in, which in some people's minds is a disadvantage. In the past few weeks I feel I have been letting myself and my team down with mistakes I shouldn't be making and so I aim to cut these mistakes out with a little help from you if it is at all possible. As you are the world's No. 1 goalkeeper, your training methods must be successful. I wonder if it would be at all possible for you to write to me explaining these so I can cut out these mistakes. As we face a top-of-the-table match on Sunday, 22nd, I would appreciate it greatly if you could send me information on your training methods as soon as possible."

Kevin, Nottingham.

"I hope that this letter finds you in good health and in fit condition. My reason for sending this letter is, apart from becoming an England Squad fan, I am also interested in becoming a good friend of yours. I wish to correspond with you . . . we can exchange ideas and get to know each other's activities . . ."

Ahmed, 25, West Malaysia.

It inevitably takes Shilton time to sift through and reply to his fan mail . . . and that in itself can generate even more letters. Take the case, finally, of the Nottingham woman, who wrote to Shilton berating him for the fact that she had not received any reply to her letters requesting two autographs for her grandson:

"I have been a widow for more than five years and, on £23 a week, I can't afford to keep throwing away stamp money to be ignored. I wish you would please oblige me Peter. I can't understand why you are the only Forest player not to have sent an autograph . . . it isn't as if I'm asking for something costly, like a goalkeeper's gloves or jersey . . ."

9

A CONVERSATION WITH ROY

Bradford City's manager Roy McFarland,
one of England's football personalities Shilton most admires.

None of the footballers Peter Shilton has played with or against since making his league debut in the mid-Sixties has made a bigger impression on him than Roy McFarland, the former Derby County and England centre-half. It is one of Shilton's biggest regrets that he and McFarland operated together on only 12 occasions in the England team. And it's one of McFarland's biggest regrets, too.

McFarland, an exceptionally skilful No. 5 whose career was hampered by serious injuries, started his career at Tranmere and spent 14 years with Derby before becoming manager of Bradford City last summer. "I would love to have played with Peter Shilton at club level," he says. "He's one of the best goalkeepers I have seen, if not *the* best, and being in the same team as him week in, week out, would have helped me become an even better player."

Shilton and McFarland were brought together again by Jason Tomas. Here's what they said:

Jason Tomas: What are the reasons for your admiration for each other?

Peter Shilton: Well, whenever I played with or against Roy, I was impressed not just by his tremendous all-round ability, but by the fact that he always gave a hundred per cent. For me, he was a great example to any youngsters in the game in that he was willing to accept the bad times as well as the good. That's the true test as far as I am concerned. Footballers are OK when things are going for them, but it's when things are going against them that you can see what they're really made of. Roy had a number of injury problems, but he was determined not to allow them to get him down. These sort of setbacks obviously affected him to a certain degree, but he battled all the way through and, even if he wasn't at his best, he still produced better performances than a lot of other players.

Roy McFarland: Even when Derby had a successful team, I always felt that we would benefit enormously through having Peter Shilton in our side. I know that Brian Clough tried to sign Peter a few times when he was manager there, and I think Clough's successor, Dave Mackay, made a bid for him, too. I talked about Peter a lot because one of his greatest assets is that he's a good talker on the field, and I appreciated that playing with him regularly would make my job that much easier. To be fair, Derby's goalkeeper, Les Green, was very good when it came to shouting advice and instructions to teammates during a match. A lot of 'keepers shout just for the sake of it, but Les did so at the right times, and was a great help to myself and the other defenders. But Peter really excelled in that department. That's why, even though we didn't play together too often, we had a good understanding.

Shilton: Not long ago, Roy and I played together in a testimonial match for Nottingham Forest's trainer Jimmy Gordon, and it was almost as if we'd been operating together for years. Afterwards, I remember thinking, "If only you could have played with Roy at club level." You know, when I played with him for England, I don't think I was as good a goalkeeper at international level as I am now. I was a bit overawed in those days, a bit immature at times. One of the things you look for in teammates is honesty, and that's one of the main reasons why I have always regretted not playing with Roy regularly. I'm not saying that the men I have played with have been dishonest, but under pressure players are inclined to say and do certain things without realising it.

McFarland: It's a fair word, that. Honesty. As a manager, one of the first things I look for in my players, apart from ability, is honesty, or rather the willingness to accept responsibility. It's all about being a good pro, and I've never come across a better pro than Peter Shilton. Our attitude to the game was basically the same, and we got on well off the field as well as on it, didn't we?

Shilton: I trusted Roy. It all comes back to that word honesty again. You know, if we went out for a couple of drinks and I said something about someone, I knew it wouldn't go any further. I don't criticise people behind their backs, but occasionally you'll make a reservation about someone during a conversation and the next thing you know, it's got back to the bloke and been distorted. I've experienced this sort of thing a few times in the past, and it's made me a bit wary of opening up to people. To be truthful, I don't trust people too much ... but I trust Roy McFarland.

Tomas: How do you differ as personalities?

McFarland: We both took our football very seriously, but him more so than me, I think. I feel I was a bit more relaxed than Peter, especially when I started being hampered by those injuries of mine. I started to view the game in a different light, and realise that there were other things in life.

Shilton: That's perfectly true. A lot of people have said that I am too intense, and over the last two or three years I've noticed this about myself, and tried to change. Because of my determination to make progress in the game, I became involved in numerous arguments and wrangles during the early part of my career. It didn't affect me in terms of my

Right, Poland's players celebrate after the 1–1 draw against England at Wembley in October 1973. That result enabled the Poles to qualify for the 1974 World Cup finals, and both Shilton and McFarland (above) – England teammates in the match – look back on it as the most disappointing experience of their careers.

performances, but I think I'd have been a lot happier, and got greater enjoyment out of the game, had I let things ride a bit more.

McFarland: Peter was rather hot-headed, and I got him going occasionally by teasing him about his lack of success at Leicester and Stoke. I gave him some terrible stick really, and he could always be relied upon to rise to the bait.

Shilton: Yes, it didn't take a lot to get me boiling. I don't know whether hot-headed is the right description, though. It was frustration more than anything. I was too impatient to win things. I didn't appreciate that, to a great extent, it's just a question of going out and playing. As I said earlier, I should have let things take their course a bit more, although it's a terribly difficult balance isn't it? I mean, if I had remained at Leicester or Stoke it's doubtful that I would have achieved anywhere near as much as I have done.

McFarland: I described Peter as hot-headed because of that occasion when he told Don Revie that he no longer wanted to be selected for the England squad. He was bitterly disappointed at being left out of the team for the 1977 British International Championship match against Scotland, after playing against Northern Ireland and Wales, and when he told me what he intended to do, Colin Todd and I tried everything to get him to change his mind. We sat with him until the early hours of the morning, striving to talk him out of it but, typical of Peter, he stood his ground and told Revie that he didn't want to be part of the England

set-up any more. I respected Peter for his honesty, but I didn't think he was right to do what he did.

Shilton: I don't know. Maybe it *wasn't* the right thing to do, but I felt I had to make my point.

Tomas: Of the England matches you played together, which ones stand out most in your memories?

McFarland: Oh, the 1–1 draw with Poland in the qualifying competition for the 1974 World Cup. It was the most depressing experience of my career – I'd set my heart on playing in the World Cup finals, and I was absolutely sick that England were bundled out of the competition in that match, especially as we created enough chances to have slaughtered the Poles.

Shilton: Yes, it was terrible. I've had a few disappointments in my career, but that was probably the biggest. I was just beginning to establish myself in the England team, and had we got to the finals I'm convinced we would have done reasonably well, and that no one, not even Ray Clemence, would have got me out of the side.

McFarland: One of Peter's England performances which stands out in my mind was the one against Scotland at Wembley in 1973. The Scots were among the few teams who were prepared to go at England at Wembley, and I'll never forget that save Peter made from Dalglish a few minutes from the end, with England leading 1–0. As soon as Dalglish hit the ball, I thought it had to be a goal. To me, Peter's save was every bit as good as the one Gordon Banks made from Pele in the 1970 World Cup.

Shilton: I played in the match against Northern Ireland at Wembley when Roy tore his Achilles tendon, the injury which more or less ended his international career. He fell awkwardly when challenging for a high ball, but the thing I particularly recall about the incident was the height he jumped. It was phenomenal, it was as if he was on a trampoline. You know, I judge players on their consistency, and when watching Roy in action for England I can't honestly ever recall him have a bad game.

Tomas: Who are the best managers you've had?

McFarland: Brian Clough and Alf Ramsey. I had enormous respect for Clough because he was so honest with his Derby players. Some managers are inclined to be a little frightened to have a go at certain players, "big-name" players, but I found that Clough treated everyone the same.

Shilton: That sums him up perfectly. You know exactly where you stand. I've been a bit annoyed at some of the comments Brian Clough has made about certain players in the Press. I think he goes over the top sometimes, but there's always an element of truth in what he says.

McFarland: Remember the 2–0 defeat by Poland in Chorzow [a 1974 World Cup qualifying tie in June 1973]? After the match, we all went up to the hotel room Bobby Moore and Alan Ball were sharing, for a few drinks, and as we were sitting there, talking about the match, in walked Alf. The England defenders like Moore and myself were explaining how we were responsible for the two Poland goals, but Alf, drinking his beer from the bottle like everyone else, would have none of it. He was maintaining that the goals had been *his* fault because he hadn't anticipated the situations leading up to them and not sorted it out in training beforehand. It was incredible – you know, we were talking before about honesty . . .

McFarland: Alf Ramsey was also very honest and straightforward with his players. The players would have died for him wouldn't they? My other England manager, Don Revie, was great to me, and I would never dream of having a go at him. But Alf was special as far as I am concerned. He turned the England squad into a sort of close-knit family through keeping faith with his players, although I have to admit that he took his loyalty towards them to the extreme. It's funny, but whereas Don Revie made too many team changes, Alf Ramsey made too few. His men had served him well, and for that reason alone he found it very difficult to dicard any of them.

Shilton: I think he struck exactly the right balance in his relationship with players. On some occasions he would mix with you socially, and on others he'd set himself apart. Players will always respect a manager who lets them know that he is the boss and keeps them on their toes. That was one of the great things about Alf.

Shilton: That's what good teams are all about. They're about players doing their jobs and admitting to their mistakes. There are plenty of men like that in English football, and I've been fortunate in having many of them in the teams I've played for. But I'm still a little envious of the goalkeepers who operated behind Roy McFarland.

McFarland at the peak of his career with Derby County. "A great example to any youngster in the game," Shilton says. "In addition to possessing outstanding technical attributes, Roy always gave 100 per cent and was willing to accept the bad times as well as the good."

10

DAY
OF THE MATCH

The end of another long, hard season –
Shilton in action for Nottingham Forest against Coventry in May 1981.

It is the eve of Nottingham Forest's last match of the 1980/81 season, a game at home to Coventry City. Peter Shilton is sprawled in an armchair, wearing a blue sweat-shirt, red tracksuit bottoms and white training shoes. He is looking back over an action-packed nine months ... and forward to a break from the game at his cottage in Bigbury.

It has been a long, hard season – a season of numerous problems for both Shilton and Forest – and even in someone with his enthusiasm for football it is easy to detect a feeling of relief that it is all coming to an end. With one eye on the TV and the other on Michael and Sam Shilton, who are using his 13-stone frame as an assault course, Shilton stretches, gives a yawn and starts talking about the "ridiculously high" number of matches he has played for the club since being signed in 1977.

Those who condemn footballers for complaining about the slog of the English League season, would almost certainly gain a more sympathetic outlook on the subject if they could spend a week with Shilton. He's a man who feels, more than most, the strain of having to play an average of two matches a week. In addition to his intense determination to produce a top-class performance in every match he is forever haunted by the fear of what might happen if he doesn't. A goalkeeper is the player who can least afford to make mistakes; in Shilton's case one of the reasons why he makes so few errors during a season is that he adopts the same competitive attitude for every match, no matter how unimportant it might appear to be.

"Some players, some *teams*, sort of just go through the motions in certain matches," he says. "But I don't believe in that – if you're right mentally and physically for the so-called smaller matches, you'll be right for the bigger games."

The philosophy goes a long way towards explaining why Shilton has mixed feelings about Forest's high number of "non-competitive" friendly and testimonial games in recent seasons.

Forest took part in 14 matches outside the recognised major competitions between July 1980 and May 1981, or 17 if one includes the World Club Cup clash with Uruguay's Nacional in Tokyo and the two European "Super Cup" ties against Spain's Valencia. This was on top of 42 matches in the Championship, six in the FA Cup, four in the League Cup and two in the European Cup. The extra games took Forest to Canada, the United States, Colombia, Holland, Switzerland, Spain and Yugoslavia. In Shilton's case the pressure of that 72-match programme in 1980/81 was made more intense by his commitments to the England team.

The strain was even greater over the same period in 1979/80 when Forest's success (they won the European Cup and League Cup) swelled their overall total of games to 82.

Shilton appreciates the need for Forest to cash in on their status in this way. The club does not have the same crowd-pulling potential of some other more famous institutions – their average home attendance last season was, for example, 25,000 but he is nevertheless disappointed Forest do not display more concern for the well-being of their players.

It was, Shilton explains, a contributory factor in his decision to ask the club for a transfer and why he was initially keen on moving to a club abroad. Clubs in other countries play considerably fewer matches than those in Britain. Thus their players not only find it easier to retain their appetite for the game but have greater opportunity to hone basic technical skills in training.

Engaged in full flow about the problems of being a top British footballer, Shilton is suddenly interrupted by a telephone call from tennis player John Lloyd. Lloyd wants to know whether Shilton will want tickets for Wimbledon, as he did the previous year. It's a reciprocal act. Lloyd himself wants tickets for one of England's close season matches at Wembley. Jon Holmes follows on the phone. He wonders if there's a chance of Shilton letting him have any FA Cup Final tickets. Almost immediately afterwards a Newmarket stable lad is on the 'phone. He draws Shilton's attention to the fact that a tip he gave the footballer for a race earlier that day had "come up trumps". The irony is that Shilton had forgotten to place a bet.

"It won by three lengths," Shilton mutters, gently reproaching himself. He thinks about it for a while and then shakes his head before turning his attention towards the match against Coventry.

It's an important match for both teams. Forest are still in with a chance of finishing high enough in the First Division to gain a place in the next season's lucrative UEFA Cup competition. Coventry are involved in a desperate battle with Sunderland, Brighton and Norwich City to avoid being relegated with Leicester and Crystal Palace. Shilton confesses that he's had a struggle to get himself right for the match after his England appearance in the World Cup qualifying tie against Rumania at Wembley two days earlier.

The result had been a 0–0 draw. It was a match England had badly wanted to win ... and came perilously close to losing as a result of a "nightmare" moment for Shilton in the first half. He had slipped over as a Rumanian forward directed a harmless-looking looping header towards his goal. He was on the floor as the ball approached him. For a moment it had looked certain to go over his head and into the net but Shilton had somehow managed to reach it with an outstretched arm and push it away.

"It was one of the best saves I've ever made," he says. "The thing is, I kept my head – if I'd have panicked and flapped at the ball, I could easily have put it straight to a Rumanian player following up."

Shilton had found it something of a nerve-wracking game. England, under enormous pressure following their previous disappointing Wembley performance, had been rarely able to find any rhythm. "It was one of those games where I had to keep total concentration," Shilton explains. "It was a bit like the Poland game in 1973 in that, although England seemed in control, you never felt really comfortable."

Shilton had had a late night to unwind and "come down the mountain a little bit". The following day, after travelling back to Nottingham in the morning, he took Sue out to lunch and had spent the afternoon and evening with his feet up at home. Then on Friday morning he had started building himself up again – for what must have seemed the umpteenth time in the season – for the match against Coventry.

Shilton is nearly always the last to arrive at the City ground for training, deliberately so. Leaving himself just enough time to get changed (10 minutes before he is due to go on the field) he can concentrate solely on what he has to do and avoids "social chit-chat". He says: "I'm not one of those players who can hang around the dressing room chatting to people. I like a laugh and giggle with the other players but not before I've done my job."

On the Friday morning before the Coventry match he is particularly uncommunicative. "I really set my stall out to get the couple of drinks I had on Wednesday night out of my system," he says. "I tried to do everything right. I dealt with shots and headers in the same way that I'd deal with them in matches, so that I could get back into what I call the groove."

Back at home the same day he adds: "Now it's just a question of me keeping in it, mentally, for the match tomorrow. I just relax on Friday night. I don't do anything. I've got to have peace and quiet. In fact, in normal circumstances, you wouldn't be here and I wouldn't be talking to you!"

Despite what's at stake for the two teams, Shilton insists that it's "just another game" to him. "It's no more important than any of the other First Division matches we've had this season," he argues. "All right, I know the result could decide whether or not we get into the UEFA Cup next season, but we shouldn't be in this position. We should have done it long before now and if we don't get the right result against Coventry tomorrow, well that will be fair enough as far as I am concerned."

On the eve of a match, Shilton says that he never really thinks about the game, nor the men who are due to oppose him. Earlier in the day, Coventry had announced that despite a fitness doubt concerning their Republic of Ireland international, Gerry Daly, they are almost certain to field an unchanged team. Shilton, though, is left scratching his head when asked to name that team and, indeed, is more than a little vague when attempting to pinpoint their key men and the system they use.

"I think about the team we're up against in general terms," he says. "I'm much more concerned with what I am going to do, and what Forest are going to do."

It's 10.30 pm and time for bed, but then there's another telephone call. This time it's from a national newspaper reporter.

Sue Shilton answers it and, non-plussed, immediately passes the 'phone to her husband.

"Ah!" says the voice at the other end. "I was just checking to make sure you were there."

"Of course I'm here," Shilton replies, "we've got a game tomorrow..."

"Yes, I know, but there's a rumour going around that you and your wife have split up and that you're staying in a hotel."

Shilton puts down the receiver. "Unbelievable!"

When Forest are at home, Shilton's Saturday routine is always basically the same. Sue gets up with the children at 8 to 8.30 am and quickly gets them dressed, fed and in front of the TV video in order that Shilton can remain peacefully in bed until 10.45 am. "That's one of the things I most enjoy about Saturday mornings," he says. "I know I've done everything right in my preparation for the match throughout the week, and I get a fantastic feeling just lying there for an hour, an hour-and-a-half, drinking a pot of tea and reading the papers (the Daily Express and The Sporting Life)."

Sue is meanwhile ironing the light-brown suit he wants to wear, complaining mildly about the lack of space in his wardrobe... and the telephone call they received late the previous night. Earlier another newspaper reporter – a local freelance whom the

Shiltons have known for a number of years – had telephoned her mother after trying in vain to get any reply from the Shiltons' home. She suspects that there was a connection between that call and the one they got from the national newspaper, and she makes a mental note to challenge the freelance reporter about it if she sees him at the match.

Sue and Shilton's father Les always sit beside each other in the stand (Shilton's mother looks after the children) and both are inclined to be very uptight during a game. "It doesn't take much for me to flare up on match days," she says. "I can't not go to watch him, but it's terrible. I think it's the position he's in more than anything."

Michael Shilton, busy sticking pictures of top footballers in a scrapbook, observes that he still hasn't been able to obtain one of West Ham and England midfield star Trevor Brooking. Sue laughs.

"Michael, who's mummy's favourite footballer apart from dad?"

"Trevor Brooking," he says, matter-of-factly.

"Oh he's nice," she says. "So quiet and well-mannered . . . if you didn't know who he was, you'd never think he was a professional footballer."

At 11am Shilton surfaces, looking immaculate in that light-brown suit, cream shirt and dark brown tie. He's a strikingly handsome figure, his impressive build and strong, swarthy features giving him the appearance of a Latin matinee idol. Apart from being one of the most successful sportsmen in Britain, he's one of the best-groomed too. His hair, naturally wavy, is permed by the well-known Stoke hairdresser John Belfield.

The style Belfield has given him, "a sort of very short Afro", once earned Shilton the "Head of the Year" award. "I think it's very natural-looking and smart," Shilton enthuses. "John just asked me one day: 'How about having your hair permed?' My immediate reaction was: 'You must be joking' . . . You know, the old-fashioned attitude towards a man having his hair permed? But he talked me into it and I've found this style tremendous. All I have to do is push my hands through it and it's in place – I feel really good with it."

Shilton's taste is also reflected in his clothes. "I like to be dressed fairly smart," he says. His suits and shirts have to be specially made to accommodate his uncommonly long arms. He usually goes to a tailor and shirtmaker in London's Savile Row.

An early touch of the ball . . . and Shilton turns it to advantage by seizing the opportunity and switching defence into attack.

When Forest are playing at home, the team have to meet at a local hotel just before midday. They have lunch and then watch TV together there before departing for the ground at around 1.45 pm. "It gives the players a feeling of togetherness," Shilton says. "Some look upon it as a bit of a bind, but I'm all for it." Before leaving his home, Shilton has a 10-minute walk in his garden, which culminates in him feeding his incinerator with unwanted post that has arrived that day and any mess that the Shiltons' labrador Julie has deposited on the lawn. "I do that every morning," he says. "It's not superstition . . . I just find it pleasant and relaxing to stretch the legs in the garden."

The 15-minute journey to the hotel starts with Shilton drawing your attention to the fact that the hedges and grass verges outside his house badly need trimming. "Must get on to the council about that . . . the rates we're paying." Suddenly he remembers something he read in the Daily Express. "Peter Taylor says that if we get into the UEFA Cup, we'll conquer Europe next season." He smiles wryly. "At the start of this season, Peter said that we'd have the Championship wrapped up by Christmas. Still I like positive thinking . . ."

Sue, who had just joined a TV video club, reminds him that after dropping him off at the hotel she has arranged to exchange the first film she's hired, "The Deerhunter", for "A Star is Born".

"Do you think it will be a bit weepy?" she asks him.

"I think so," he replies with a wink. "I think you'll like it."

In the dressing room before a match, Shilton spends five minutes doing warming-up exercises and then, when he's changed into his kit, he likes to sit quietly by himself. "I've gone through all my nervousness and excitement, and I just need to sit down relaxed and have a nice cup of tea."

He goes out, onto the field in second position, behind Forest's captain John McGovern, and sprints almost flat out into the penalty area. There he hits a ball as hard as he can into the empty net. "Sometimes. I'll whack it too hard and miss the bloody goal," he says. "Honestly! It's ridiculous! But when I do that, I know that I'm probably a little bit too excited and will make a conscious effort to calm down."

Forest's substitute – against Coventry it is Peter Ward – gives him a "feel" of the ball during the

Forest 0–1 and Shilton is beaten in the 25th minute (opposite page) when a Tom English shot hits the post, only for Garry Thompson (on the ground) to pounce on the rebound and hit a low shot into the corner of the net.

Above left, how did *that* happen and who was to blame? "I think I could have saved it," Shilton insisted afterwards. "I didn't feel 100 per cent in the early stages of the game ... really, had the shot come later, I feel I probably *would* have saved it."

Above right, Shilton's mood of disappointment and frustration suddenly changes to one of determination. "I'm thinking: 'Well, it's happened ... let's get on with the game.' I'm a very stubborn person and this helps me a lot as a footballer. You know, there's no way I'm going to accept defeat until the final whistle."

kick-in with a succession of soft shots from the penalty spot and crosses from the flanks.

Finally, just before the kick-off, Shilton sprints back and forth across the D on the edge of his box and starts clapping his hands and shouting at the other Forest defenders.

When Forest's left-back Frank Gray looks towards him, Shilton punches a fist into his hand ("Frank can be a little weak in his tackling occasionally") and makes signs and gestures to Bryn Gunn and Einar Jan Aas. "The only man I don't do this sort of thing to before a match is Kenny Burns. I'll shout at him during a match, but he's made it clear that he doesn't want me to gee him up beforehand. That's fair enough ... all players are different and therefore you've got to treat them differently."

Only sitting by Shilton's goal can an outsider properly appreciate the influence he has on his teams, how his personality and presence pays off. "He's the most vocal goalkeeper in the League," remarks a photographer, whose countless Saturday afternoons spent huddled alongside the City Ground goals make him something of an expert on the subject. "He's the one who really makes this lot tick."

Coventry are by now on the attack 20 yards from Shilton's goal. Mindful of the danger of them pushing Forest's defenders deep into his penalty area Shilton shouts: "Hold ... Hold ...." Gunn gets in a tackle and, unaware of a Coventry man coming up fast behind him, starts to dwell on the ball. "Bryn ... Away." Then Forest get a corner and as Burns shapes to move forward into the edge of the penalty area, leaving only Aas marking Tom English on the half-way line, Shilton pulls him back. "No Kenny, No . . . ."

Coventry take the lead in the 25th minute when Garry Thompson, involved in an abrasive physical battle with Burns, wins an Andy Blair cross and flicks it on for English, who produces a magnificent turn and swerving shot which hits a post. Thompson, following up, seizes on the rebound on the right and drives a low shot low into the far corner. John Robertson puts Forest level from a penalty towards the end of the first half, and that's how the score remains, despite a second half in which both teams have enough chances to win fairly comfortably.

It is an extraordinary half for Shilton. The Coventry Evening Telegraph chronicles the moments that Coventry beat Forest's defence – but fail to get the ball past the man in goal.

". . . A glorious ball from Hunt sent Roberts galloping through on the overlap down the left. But his first-time centre was tipped away for a corner by Shilton as Thompson challenged . . . Then a magnificent move from City in the 61st minute could well have brought a goal. Hunt began it out on the left and when the move continued along the right, first English and then Blair twisted Forest's defence inside out before Daly brought Shilton to a diving save . . . With 12 minutes to go, City missed a great chance of the second goal. English beat the offside trap with a great run up the right, out-pacing Burns, and then found Thompson with a first-time centre. But with the goal at his mercy, the big striker (suffering from Shilton-itis?) lost his balance as he tried a right-foot volley and Forest scrambled the ball to safety . . . Four minutes from the end it took a great save from Shilton to stop Gillespie scoring after a brilliant solo effort from the defender . . ."

In Forest's Jubilee Social Club afterwards, Shilton is flanked by Sue and Les Shilton. Still perspiring, he agrees that Coventry's goal stemmed from slipshod marking by his defenders. "They can be a bit slow to react to situations sometimes because I think they're saying to themselves: 'Oh well, Peter will save it anyway.' You know, to some extent, I feel they can rely too much on me instead of taking the initiative themselves."

Even so, a perfectionist to the last, he still reckons he could have prevented the goal. "I didn't feel 100 per cent in the early stages of the game, I don't know why . . . it was probably a reaction from Wednesday's England game. Not only this, today's game was a bit scrappy in the first half and I found it difficult to get into it. Really, had that shot come later in the game, I feel I would probably have saved it. There's a very thin line between what's possible and what's impossible. The fact that I concern myself so much with that thin line is possibly what makes me different to other goalkeepers."

Sue Shilton's attention is suddenly drawn towards the freelance journalist who telephoned her mother the previous day.

"How are you Sue?" he asks with a wave.

"Ask my mother," she replies. "You shouldn't ring my mum."

"Oh, I thought she'd like to have a chat . . ."

"Not to a journalist she wouldn't."

Shilton tries to interject a touch of humour into the exchange. "Do you fancy her or something," he asks the journalist, with a laugh.

"Oh, it was just a chat," he replies, blushing, "I wouldn't dream of using anything she said to me."

"You better not," Sue retorts, fixing him with a menacing stare, which breaks into a forgiving smile.

On the car journey from the ground, Shilton is studying the First Division table. Coventry have escaped relegation, at the expense of Norwich, while Nottingham Forest's slender chance of getting into the UEFA Cup now rests with Southampton's result in their last match of the season, against Ipswich the following week (they won 3–2). He notes that Forest finished 10 points behind the champions, Aston Villa, and lists the matches in which his team might easily have closed the gap. "If I stay at this club," he says, defiantly, "I'll help us win the Championship."

Shilton had asked Forest for a transfer, but there seemed some doubt about whether Clough was as prepared to let him go as he'd initially intimated.

Over the ensuing weeks Shilton himself began to have second thoughts about leaving, particularly if it meant going to a Continental club. He decided that if he was to be presented with a fresh challenge it would have to be in England. His ambition is to become a manager at the end of his playing career and among the clubs willing to give him the chance to broaden himself as a footballer were Tottenham, Everton and Manchester United. United reportedly offered Forest two players, Gary Bailey and Garry Birtles, in exchange for Shilton and Trevor Francis. But Shilton was particularly enthusiastic about Tottenham's bid for him. Apart from the prospect of being able to lose himself in such a big, cosmopolitan city such as London, he felt he could make a big contribution to a Tottenham team well known for its vulnerability in defence.

But against all this, Shilton was caught in a

financial dilemma. Forest were asking at least £500,000 for Shilton. He felt he'd be "stupid" to leave the club at that stage without receiving a reasonable percentage of the transfer fee on top of his salary. Forest would be making a big profit on him and if he were to remain there until the end of his contract in 1983, they'd be forced by the freedom-of-contract regulations to give him a free transfer.

"It might seem a bit mercenary," Shilton said, "but while I like winning medals as much as anyone, what really counts at the end of your playing career is how much money you've got in the bank. It's important to me that I have some financial security when I retire, because I want to be a manager and I don't want to be in a position where I can't do the job my way. A manager can be at the mercy of directors if he's doing the job because he needs the money. That's not for me."

Shilton, in fact, has set his sights on eventually

Nottingham Forest make it 1–1 through a John Robertson penalty just before half-time – but Coventry continue to create problems for Shilton and his defence.

becoming manager of the England team. He does not accept that the incredibly high standards he sets for himself and those around him, together with his apparent unwillingness to compromise in any way, might work against him. But he acknowledges the problem.

"It's an annoying part of me – something inside me which won't tolerate second best. I don't want people to expect unbelievable things from me but, at the same time, I expect unbelievable things from myself. Still, I like to think that I'm learning to temper my beliefs and channel them in the right directions."

Key to introductory picture gallery

● Debut for Stoke at Wolves in November 1974. Stoke drew 2–2 and went on to finish fifth in the League Championship.

● Cheers for a save. Not only strikers win plaudits. Forest fans express as much joy for a Shilton shut-out.

● The general, marshalling his troops at Stoke, Leicester and Nottingham Forest. "Some of my best matches are those where I don't have a shot to stop."

● Forest are through to the 1979 European Cup Final. They have beaten Cologne 1–0, thanks to an Ian Bowyer (left) goal and a great Shilton save in the final minute of the match.

Picture Credits

● Some you win, some you lose. Shilton, in full flight for Leicester against West Ham, in the Seventies. But West Ham won 5–2!

● The Shilton presence. "I take on a lot of responsibility," says Shilton, "and I expect my defenders in front of me to do the same."

● Big but as sharp and as agile as a cat. Striving to get to shots other goalkeepers don't reach. "I go flat out for everything."